Models for a Multicultural Church

Models for a Multicultural Church

Five Motives That Shape Your Church's Cross-Cultural Engagement

Kenneth Nehrbass
and **Eunice Hong**

Baker Academic
a division of Baker Publishing Group
Grand Rapids, Michigan

Published by Baker Academic
a division of Baker Publishing Group
Grand Rapids, Michigan
BakerAcademic.com

Printed in the United States of America

Library of Congress Cataloging-in-Publication Data
Names: Nehrbass, Kenneth author | Hong, Eunice author
Title: Models for a multicultural church : five motives that shape your church's cross-cultural engagement / Kenneth Nehrbass and Eunice Hong.
Description: Grand Rapids, Michigan : Baker Academic, a division of Baker Publishing Group, [2026] | Includes bibliographical references and index. | Audience term: Clergy
Identifiers: LCCN 2026007718 | ISBN 9781540970817 paperback | ISBN 9781493456277 ebook | ISBN 9781493456284 pdf
Subjects: LCSH: Christianity and culture | Multiculturalism—Religious aspects—Christianity | Ethnicity—Religious aspects—Christianity | Church work with minorities | Church growth | Pastoral theology | LCGFT: Instructional and educational works
Classification: LCC BR115.C8 N444 2026
LC record available at https://lccn.loc.gov/2026007718

The qualitative study was approved by the Institutional Review Board at California Baptist University. IRB #042-2425-EXM.

Icons in this book are from The Studio / Shutterstock.com

Cover design by Sarah Kvam

Baker Publishing Group publications use paper produced from sustainable forestry practices and postconsumer waste whenever possible.

26 27 28 29 30 31 32 7 6 5 4 3 2 1

To our families

Contents

Foreword

DERWIN L. GRAY

The gospel of King Jesus takes a wrecking ball of grace and tears down sin-built walls that divide people from God and from one another. The blood of Jesus glues separated people back to God and to one another, creating a new family made up of every tribe, tongue, and nation. God does this because he made a promise to give Abraham a multiethnic family. Jesus, the seed of Abraham, is the promise keeper, and it is through his wondrous life, sacrificial substitutionary death on the cross, and glorious resurrection that this new family is birthed.

The Father's colorful new society is called the church, the body of Christ, the bride of Christ, which exists to reflect his glory on earth. Yet the journey toward becoming an authentic multiethnic church is exhausting and frustrating. It requires deep theological reflection, gospel-intentionality, sacrificial love, reliance on the Spirit, and humility. Simply put, it requires a deep gospel understanding that produces deep discipleship lived out. A fragile, weak, shallow disciple need not apply. It's too hard. The spiritual warfare is too robust, and the zeitgeist is a strong wind, constantly blowing against the mighty few who take this gospel challenge. But I testify that it can be done. It was done in the early church, and it's being done at Transformation Church, where I serve as cofounder and lead pastor.

That's why this book is so important! It does something that too few resources do: It gives voice to the everyday church members. Too often, conversations about multiethnic ministry focus solely on pastors and church leaders. But what about the people in the pews? What are their experiences, their struggles, and their hopes? If we want to be a church that truly reflects the kingdom of God, we need to hear from everyone. This book does just that.

At the same time, this book isn't just about stories; it's also about solutions. By incorporating the voices of church members, it provides practical insights for pastors and leaders seeking to cultivate a gospel-shaped multiethnic church. It doesn't just diagnose the challenges; it offers a way forward. Additionally, this book fills a crucial gap in academic literature. Too often the "why" behind different cross-cultural postures in the church is overlooked. This book provides an important framework to help us understand the factors that shape these postures, giving both scholars and practitioners a clearer picture of what's at stake.

Ultimately, my prayer is that this book will do more than inform—it will transform. May it stir pastors, leaders, and church members alike to lean into the hard, holy work of building a multiethnic church. May it remind us that the gospel is bigger than our preferences, our fears, and our past. And may it move us closer to the glorious vision of Revelation 7:9: a church where every nation, tribe, people, and language worship together as one.

Introduction

Goals for This Book

At the end of this book, you should know

- the five MOTIVEs that impact a church's cross-cultural posture (Multiculturality, Oneness, Togetherness, Inclusionary Vision, and Ethnic Diversity)
- the differences between the cross-cultural postures found among churches

You should be able to

- assess a church's cross-cultural posture with the Cross-Cultural Posture Assessment Tool (CPAT)
- evaluate the strengths and weaknesses of each cross-cultural posture
- apply the values in this book to help churches develop their cross-cultural ministry

You should value

- multiple culturally patterned expressions of worship
- cultural differences in leadership

You should empathize with

- reasons why people may prefer a monocultural worship experience
- reasons why people may prefer a multicultural worship experience

Altars are the most sacred spaces in churches. They represent the most intimate acts of worship where we encounter God. Altars are where offerings are made, the bread and wine are made ready for Communion, and new believers are summoned to make a profession of faith. Because the Israelites valued their worship experience so tremendously, they protected their altar from outsiders, to keep anything from defiling it (Heb. 9:7–10).

Churches also have figurative "altars"—the things they cherish so deeply that they have a hard time sharing them with others: finances, pulpit time, worship styles, even the kitchen! I (Ken) was on the leadership team at a church that shared its facilities with a group of much lower socioeconomic status, and members of the richer congregation left sticky notes all over the kitchen with instructions for how to behave in this "sacred space."

The research presented in this book is about churches that take the bold step to share their altars—both figuratively and literally. Who are these people who worship, pray, and serve with those who come from backgrounds different from their own? What are people's experiences in these multicultural or multiethnic churches?

Last Sunday at 11:00 a.m., three thousand Christians from various ethnic backgrounds worshiped in the English service at The Grove Community Church in Riverside, California, while The Grove Español met down the hall in the gymnasium-sized youth building. Both pastors preached on the same topic but had different preaching styles. Meanwhile, sixty miles west of The Grove, a declining predominantly White church called The Fount completed its 9:00 a.m. English service and rented out its sanctuary to a burgeoning Vietnamese congregation at 11:00 a.m., while renting out its east chapel (formerly the youth building) to a Spanish-speaking congregation. And up in Beaverton, Oregon, the weekly service at Village Church took a more radical approach of multiculturality by combining worship in Spanish, Korean, and English in the *same* service! These three churches have very different ways of being "multicultural." And these aren't the only approaches. Just east of The Grove, Centerpoint Church in Colton, California, has a monocultural English worship service that attracts many second- and third-generation Latinos who are no longer learning Spanish at home. And just to the west of Centerpoint, Fellowship Church in Monrovia intentionally cultivates interracial friendships.

Clearly, churches' cross-cultural postures vary significantly, and the variation cannot be explained simply by the demographics of the town where a church is located. Within ten miles of my (Ken's) home in Riverside, California, there are monocultural/monoethnic churches, multiethnic churches, churches that rent out space to newly arrived immigrants, and churches that focus on racial reconciliation. As researchers in the social sciences, we wanted to discover factors that explain the different approaches that churches have for crossing cultural and ethnic boundaries. And as ordained pastors, our goal was to translate these insights into "best practices" for leaders who engage in (or want to engage in) multicultural or multiethnic ministry. While we acknowledge that no single cross-cultural posture in this book is inherently better than another, our aim is to help leaders identify which posture represents their church today and determine what steps should be taken to better fulfill their specific calling, within their context, to minister to their constituency.

Our Methods

When we began casting our vision for the book, people told us they thought that their congregation fit the criteria for our study but wondered aloud, "I don't know how you are defining 'multicultural.'" We weren't sure either, and it took quite some time to iron out the definitions as we now have them below. At first, we figured our main criteria should be churches that fit Michael Emerson's "80 percent rule": No single ethnicity would represent more than 80 percent of the congregation.[1] This was *one* of our inclusion criteria, but it turned out that there are other marks of ethnic diversity, and there are other motives driving churches' cross-cultural postures beyond just ethnic diversity (see part 1). Should our criteria include only churches that use more than one language? Would those language groups need to be in a combined worship service or could they be separate?

1. Emerson, *People of the Dream*, 35.

Ultimately, to select research sites for this book, we started with a "purposeful sampling" approach that qualitative researchers refer to as "Maximum Variation Sampling."[2] We asked people in the multiethnic, multicultural church movement to help us compile a list of possible sites. We considered churches in the United States that were known—either to us personally or by reputation—to be multicultural or multiethnic. We then selected sites that were different from one another: ones that were multilingual, ones that were multiethnic but not multilingual, ones where the church rented out space to a congregation of a different ethnicity, ones that expressly addressed issues of race, and ones that avoided the topic. Once we had chosen fifteen sites, we visited those churches and reached out to church leaders and members of the congregations for interviews. We interviewed sixty-two church leaders and members to understand people's experiences in multiethnic and multicultural churches.[3] The narratives shared in the following pages reflect the experiences of members who attend and those who lead churches with various cross-cultural postures. Minor adjustments have been made to some of the interview responses in the interest of readability and clarity.

Note that we have used pseudonyms for the laypeople we interviewed to protect their privacy. However, we felt that there is value in providing the real names of the churches, because they are doing innovative things to reach out across cultures. Because a quick web search will turn up the names of the pastoral leadership at those churches, we have (with their permission) retained the real names of the paid staff at churches mentioned in this book.

The insights from these interviews provide a deeper understanding of the challenges and opportunities faced by multiethnic/multicultural churches. Once we understood the motives that drive various cross-cultural postures, we were able to develop a Cross-Cultural Posture Assessment Tool. We deployed this quantitative instrument[4] to 214 participants to test the tool for reliability and validity, and to ensure that it was user-friendly (see the end of part 1).

2. Palinkas et al., "Purposeful Sampling," 18.

3. The qualitative study was approved by the Institutional Review Board at California Baptist University. IRB #042-2425-EXM.

4. The quantitative study was approved by the Institutional Review Board at California Baptist University. IRB #110-2425-EXM.

Definitions

Church leaders do not seem to agree on what is meant by a "multicultural church" or "multiethnic church" (although they do seem to agree that achieving such a vision is difficult—but not impossible). Before delving into the motives that influence churches' cross-cultural postures, we list here terms and definitions as they are used in this book:

- **Race:** A social construct whereby people are separated and categorized based on physical characteristics (i.e., skin color, eye color, hair type, facial features). Racial categories like those used by the US Census Bureau (White, Black or African American, American Indian or Alaska Native, Asian, and Native Hawaiian or Other Pacific Islander) do not sufficiently capture the significant variations of ancestral backgrounds found in churches or in wider society. Therefore, here we try to use the terms "ethnicity," "multiethnic," and "ethnic diversity" (defined further below) rather than "race," "multiracial," and "racial diversity." However, because the term "ethnic reconciliation" is rarely employed, we do use the term "racial reconciliation."
- **Racial reconciliation:** A process of forgiving hurts caused by racism (usually at the systemic level) and advocating for the rights of people of all ethnicities.
- **Ethnicity:** "A cultural group with common links such as biology, heritage, language, religion, and geography or migration patterns."[5]
- **Multiethnic:** A group that is ethnically diverse. For this study, this term specifically refers to a group that has people from various national or ancestral backgrounds gathered together. If the different cultural patterns of this group are actually represented, the group is also "multicultural" (see below).
- **Monoethnic:** It is impossible for an organization to be truly monoethnic; compare any two families, and they will have different ethnic backgrounds in the mix. Here, a monoethnic

5. Branson and Martínez, *Churches, Cultures and Leadership*, 86. See also Gushiken, "Christian Identity," 34; Cornell and Hartmann, *Ethnicity and Race*, 19–21.

context is one where over 80 percent of people are from a single ethnic group.

- **Multicultural:** The representation of multiple cultures within a society or organization. Usually, this includes a variety of subcultures including race, gender, ethnicity, sexual orientation, age, socioeconomic status, physical and mental abilities, and faith traditions. However, for the purposes of this book, we specifically use the term "multicultural" to refer to a group that represents a variety of cultural patterns from people of different ethnolinguistic backgrounds (specifically, the music styles, preaching styles, and leadership styles from various cultures).
- **Monocultural:** An approach where one culture is predominantly represented.
- **Diversity:** The extent to which a variety of backgrounds are represented within a single group. In today's parlance, this term includes a variety of characteristics including racial, gender, ethnic, sexual, age, and socioeconomic diversity as well as diverse physical and mental abilities, and even faith traditions. Because this book focuses on different cross-cultural postures in churches, we limit our inquiry of diversity to ethnic diversity, which is described below.
- **Ethnic diversity:** For this study, we contrast ethnic diversity with multiculturality by limiting the meaning of ethnic diversity to the extent to which people from various national or ancestral backgrounds are gathered together in a single group. Their ancestral cultural patterns may or may not be observable but are likely under the surface. If the different cultural patterns of this ethnically diverse group are actually represented, the group is also "multicultural" (see above).

Ken's Entrance into Multicultural Church Ministry

I (Ken) remember my first consciously cross-cultural encounter. I was in middle school and was walking on a major street in Huntington Beach, California. A man asked me, in Spanish, how to get to the beach. Because I had taken a semester of Spanish by that point, I was able to answer him, "Sigue este calle" (Follow this street). He seemed to understand, and I was hooked! Not long after this, my youth group traveled across the southern border. Somehow, I felt—even though I'd never been to Mexico before—that I was home. Not that Mexico was home, but I knew I was called to cross-cultural ministry. This heterophily (as I came to learn it is called) eventually led me and my wife to spend ten years on the island of Tanna, in the nation of Vanuatu, where we worked with the local church to translate the New Testament into a minority language called Nivhaar. In that South Pacific nation we were part of an international church, and I regularly preached in two languages (Bislama and Nivhaar) on an island that was basically monoethnic (Melanesian) but where multiple languages were used for singing, prayer, Bible reading, and sermons.

Working with the church in various languages and cultures has emotionally impacted me. I've had experiences where the words of the Bible leapt off the page to me as I read in Nivhaar, or where I felt like I joined the heavenly choir when I worshiped at a Chinese church (even though I don't speak Mandarin), or where the poetic lyrics of "Danzando,"[6] a worship song, touched my heart in a way that English could not. I don't have a sound system that can play this song as loud as it was meant to be performed! Perhaps the lyrics alone are not enough to move you, but if you find yourself dancing along with hundreds of other believers, the Latin rhythms and trumpet riffs may transport your heart and mind not just to South America but to God's throne.

I realize that not everyone has these same sorts of transcendental experiences as they cross cultures. But there is a strong movement of churches that, for various practical or theological reasons, desire greater degrees of intercultural connection.

For the past twenty-five years, I have been part of multicultural churches. I was on staff at a church that shares its space with Spanish, Vietnamese, and Cambodian congregations, then I served as a missionary in the South Pacific, and now I am a member of a multiethnic church that also has a Spanish-speaking congregation. The

6. D'Clario et al., "Danzando."

relationships I've made across cultures in these churches have enriched me and have compelled me to understand more about multiethnic and multicultural congregations.

Eunice's Entrance into Multicultural Church Ministry

I (Eunice) was born in Southern California but grew up in a very traditional Korean home. Although we lived in the United States, we were surrounded by all things Korean—the news, music, food, friends, community, church, bank, and even the dry cleaners. When I started elementary school, I had to take ESL (English as a Second Language) classes because I didn't speak any English! Growing up, I learned to navigate between two very different cultures. Cultural norms and expectations that should have been "simple" were often anything but. For example, should I make eye contact with elders when they speak to me? Is it rude to take seconds or is it rude not to?

When I was ten years old, my parents were called to serve as missionaries in East Africa. Before I knew it, I found myself at a boarding school overlooking the beautiful Rift Valley, surrounded by friends from all over the world. After five formative years on the mission field, we returned to the United States, where I struggled with severe reverse culture shock and went through a period of trying to understand my cultural identity yet again.

Those younger years were challenging, to say the least, but they taught me to appreciate the beauty found in every culture. As I grew older, however, I realized that these cultural values and norms, though beautiful, can also lead to tensions and conflicts. This realization inspired me to pursue a PhD in intercultural studies.

I still firmly believe that every culture is beautiful, and it is even more beautiful when cultures come together—such as in the multicultural church! However, I also find myself grappling with some questions. For instance, how have churches navigated cultural tensions and differences to create a truly multicultural community? And despite the wealth of literature on the *why* and *how* of building a multicultural church, what do congregation members actually feel, think, and experience when they come together to worship with people from different cultures? These are some of the questions we hope to explore through the stories and narratives of those who attend multicultural churches.

What You Will Find Here

Clearly, churches' cross-cultural postures vary significantly due to their calling, context, and constituency. Why the variation? Some studies have focused on pastors' experiences leading multiracial churches, and other studies have recounted specific churches' journeys toward multiculturality. But less has been done to understand laypeople's experiences in these churches, and no theory has been previously developed to explain motives that contribute to a church's cross-cultural posture.

We discovered that churches' cross-cultural postures are affected by five motives that formulate into an apt acronym:

M **Multiculturality**: The worship service and other programming incorporate various cultures.

O **Oneness**: The church has a single organizational structure for all cultural groups.

T **Togetherness**: The church has all language and cultural groups worshiping and meeting together.

I V **Inclusionary Vision**: The church is intentional about inclusion of various ethnicities and cultures.

E **Ethnic Diversity**: The church includes people from various ethnic backgrounds.

We discuss these five MOTIVEs in part 1. Ultimately, a church's posture need not be static. Church leaders can use the Cross-Cultural Posture Assessment Tool at the end of part 1 to measure their responses to these motives so they can develop a strategic plan for where they want to guide their church next.

Part 2 describes various ways that churches leverage these five MOTIVEs to arrive at one of seven cross-cultural postures:

1. Shared-Space Posture
2. Monocultural/Monoethnic Posture
3. Advocate Posture
4. Multiethnic Posture
5. Language-Group Posture
6. Reconciling Posture
7. Culture-Blending Posture

Churches where more than 80 percent of the congregation is from a single ethnicity, and where only one culture is represented, have a monocultural/monoethnic posture. An advocate posture describes churches that are predominantly monoethnic but are deeply committed to addressing issues of racial reconciliation. Churches with the reconciling posture also have this deep commitment to diversity but have achieved the goal of becoming ethnically diverse. In churches with a shared-space posture, different language and cultural groups are present, but they remain largely separated in terms of vision, finances, events, worship services, and leadership. Churches that have a single vision, budget, and leadership team for all of the language and culture groups but that designate specific campuses or worship times to target specific ethnic groups have a language-group posture. The culture-blending posture is found in churches that have a single leadership team and budget, reaching various cultural groups that worship together regularly by blending various languages and worship and leadership styles.

Part 2 evaluates the advantages and disadvantages of each of these postures. We include observations from churches across the United States that hold these various postures, and we hope that you will find inspiration from the various approaches. We also hope you will find a way to avoid some of the pitfalls these churches have encountered.

PART 1

Five MOTIVEs That Contribute to Cross-Cultural Postures

No two churches approach cross-cultural engagement in the same way. While much has been written about becoming multicultural and about pastors' experiences leading these churches, far less attention has been given to the experiences of laypeople within these congregations. In addition, no comprehensive theory has yet been developed to explain the motives that shape a church's cross-cultural posture. We seek to address these gaps.

In the course of our research, we discovered that churches define "multicultural" in markedly different ways. In this section, we clarify the various dimensions of multicultural churches by explaining each of the five MOTIVEs that shape a church's cross-cultural posture: Multiculturality, Oneness, Togetherness, Inclusionary Vision, and Ethnic Diversity. Finally, we introduce a cross-cultural posture assessment tool designed to help churches assess their current cross-cultural posture.

CHAPTER 1

Multiculturality

The time is coming to gather all nations and tongues. And they shall come and shall see my glory.

—Isaiah 66:18

Chapter Goals

By the end of this chapter, you should be able to do the following:

- describe how the term "multicultural" is different from "multiethnic"
- identify marks of multiculturality
- reflect on the level of multiculturality in your own congregation

"Multiculturality" refers to the extent to which multiple cultures and/or languages are represented in a church's worship, sermons, and leadership styles. Do you hear worship songs in different languages? Are the sermons translated? Does the church celebrate holidays from different cultures?

Note that while churches are increasingly multiethnic, far fewer are multicultural. Having ethnic diversity in a church (discussed further in chap. 5) does not necessarily result in multiculturality. Many multiethnic churches are monocultural in that they have a single language, single worship style, and single leadership style. Note this does not mean that congregants *necessarily* assimilate to the majority White culture in the United States—at times, a sort of "third culture" is created.

Similarly, the number of nationalities represented in a church does little to indicate how much those various cultures are represented in the worship experience at the church.[1] A church may be highly international but still monocultural in leadership, programming, and worship style.

If multiculturality refers to the representation of different cultures, then multicultural*ism*, like all "isms," is an ideological commitment to this representation. Within the evangelical church, multiculturalism is a commitment to representing multiple cultures so that God gets the glory and so people are welcomed and exposed to the gospel in a way that they can understand best.

Unfortunately, "multiculturalism" has become one of those controversial buzzwords, as some Christian thinkers have feared that inclusivity is at odds with the exclusionary claims of Scripture.[2] That is, does embracing other cultures cause us to water down the gospel?

Manuel Ortiz attempted to allay these fears by arguing that multiculturalism can be redeemed if the goal is grounded in biblical truth rather than relativism: "The goal of multiculturalism should not be increased cultural sensitivity or inclusivism so that no one is locked outside the gate. . . . Rather, it should be to see the church, by way of multiethnicity, inclusivism and cultural sensitivity, bring about biblical reconciliation, justice and righteousness in the church and in society."[3]

Note that Ortiz seems to justify multiculturalism only insofar as its ultimate end is "biblical reconciliation, justice and righteousness." But he seems to be giving in to a false dichotomy here. Multiculturality is capable of achieving biblical reconciliation, justice, and

1. Kwiyani, *Multicultural Kingdom*, 118.
2. Dieppe, "What's Wrong with Multiculturalism?"
3. Ortiz, *One New People*, 60.

righteousness *as well as* the biblical ends of cultural sensitivity and inclusivity (1 Cor. 9:19–23). These are *all* biblically grounded values within Christian ministry, as long as they are all achieved while still adhering to the doctrinal truths found in Scripture. In fact, in addition to the biblical values of reconciliation, justice, righteousness, sensitivity, and inclusivity, we have identified these benefits of multiculturality within the church:

1. **People get a taste of "heaven on earth":** God is most glorified when the eschatological vision of all cultures worshiping together is realized.[4]
2. **Hospitality to our neighbors:** People feel most comfortable worshiping in a language that is familiar to them.[5]
3. **Contextualization:** People respond best to the gospel when it is communicated in a way that "makes sense" to their culture. As Paul Mbandi points out, when Christ became one of us, he did not lose any of his identity as God (Phil. 2:6).[6] If the incarnation is a metaphor for ministry, we do not ask people from other cultures to give up their identities when they join our fellowships. This is the heartbeat of multiculturality.
4. **Exposure:** We grow when we are introduced to multicultural hermeneutics, various leadership styles, and various worship styles.[7]

In the church, multiculturalism is a commitment to representing the Christian gospel in and through all cultures. It resists our tendency to separate into silos. In an act of subverting Donald McGavran's much-discussed Homogenous Unit Principle (HUP),[8] Harvey Kwiyani coined the term "heterogeneous unit principle" to describe the

4. Patten, *Leading a Multicultural Church*, 164–65. See also Williams and Jones, *In Church as It Is in Heaven*.

5. Rhodes, *Where the Nations Meet*, 21–34.

6. Mbandi, "Unity of the Church," 163.

7. Tennent, *World Christianity*, 1–24.

8. Nehrbass, *Advanced Missiology*, 215–19.

church's commitment to multiculturality.[9] This HUP 2.0 values *difference*. It maintains that churches benefit when multiple cultural value orientations, thought patterns, languages, and styles are found together.

Below we describe five marks of multiculturality in churches.

Worship Songs Are in More Than One Language Each Sunday

Churches with high multiculturality incorporate the various languages spoken by members of the congregation. Note that multilingualism is not the sine qua non of a multicultural church, but it is "an inevitable and integral part" of such a church.[10] In these churches, different languages are seen as assets or "value added." As Jonathan Downie explains, we need to stop seeing languages as barriers and see them as blessings.[11]

Worship can be multilingual in various ways. For example:

- Sing a song that was written in another language known by some members of the congregation that represents the music style of that culture. Translate the chorus into a language the congregation knows best.
- Sing an English song, but translate some key words into another language (or languages) known by some members of the congregation.

There is a growing bank of popular worship songs originally written in English and then professionally produced in Spanish, and worship leaders can find those translations on the internet in order to incorporate some of those lyrics. For example, in 2012, Hillsong Church released nine versions of its album *Global Project*—in Spanish, Portuguese, Korean, Mandarin, Indonesian, German, French, Swedish, and Russian. And Proskuneo Ministries recently released its album *Feast of Praise* in fourteen languages.[12] Additionally, we

9. Kwiyani, *Multicultural Kingdom*, 132.
10. Choi, "Multicultural Church," 14.
11. Downie, *Multilingual Church*.
12. Proskuneo Ministries, *Feast of Praise*.

have now reached a point where AI can fairly successfully translate English praise song lyrics into other major languages without awkward phrasing. But longtime members of Village Church—a highly multicultural church in Beaverton, Oregon—remember a time when all lyrics had to be translated by someone at the church. And in fact, in many cases, they still do this as they prepare each Sunday.

Language is not the only domain where cultural differences show up. Even in English there are many possible cultures that can be represented in worship. I (Ken) had no idea that bluegrass worship music existed until I visited Drakes Branch Baptist Church in rural Virginia. The church had supported me and my wife when we were missionaries in the nation of Vanuatu, and they invited me to fly to Virginia to speak about our Bible translation work. In addition to playing the contemporary praise choruses and hymns, the worship band incorporated a banjo and stand-up bass. The inclusion of bluegrass was not tokenism, and it wasn't reserved for a special occasion. It was natural for this community to include a style of worship that was familiar to them.

Here are examples of worship styles from around the world:

- Caribbean (Chevelle Franklyn)
- West African (Joe Mettle)
- South African (Benjamin Dube)
- Russian (Darina Kochanzhi)
- Gospel (Kirk Franklin, CeCe Winans)
- Native American (Jonathan Maracle)
- Indonesian (JPCC Worship)

Note that for a church to have high multiculturality, there will be multiple languages and worship styles, but various groups may not be worshiping *together*. ("Togetherness" is described in chap. 3.) Many churches have high multiculturality and low togetherness. For example, the Spanish service is held separately from the English one. This high multiculturality and low togetherness results in the language-group posture (chap. 10). A church that worships in various languages *together* is a special breed: the culture-blending posture (chap. 12).

Pastoral Leadership Styles Represent More Than One Cultural Background

Cultures have different leadership styles, and a church with high multiculturality represents these various styles. For example, the Anglo pastoral leadership style has been described as less hierarchical and consensus-based, whereas more top-down approaches are found in Korean[13] and Hispanic[14] churches. Antonio, a church musician from Colombia whom we interviewed for this book, described his own observations of the different leadership styles.

> Another challenge to our mindset as evangelicals in Latin America is that the church belongs to the pastor. In America, you don't have that. I feel this is better in many ways. . . . You have a group of elders that cover the main pastor and his associate pastors, and his responsibility is mostly teaching and preaching—not necessarily shepherding during the week. . . . You have the elders, you have the pastor that is covered by them, you have the leadership, and you have the congregation. In Latin America, it's upside down. Most of the time you don't have elders. It's the pastor and his family.

On the other hand, Antonio believes that pastors from South America are likely to focus on maintaining good relationships with the congregation:

> In Latin America, the pastor is not as worried about composing a great sermon; rather he focuses on spending time during the week shepherding his community. He's in relationship with the community: going to the hospital, going to the problems, listening to all the things like that. . . . The pastor has to smell more like the sheep in the congregation than a microphone. [That is, he must spend more time with the "sheep" than he does preaching into the microphone.] So there has to be a balance.

The balance includes the various culturally patterned emphases of professionalism and relationships, hierarchy and plurality. Antonio

13. Edwards and Kim, *Estranged Pioneers*, 54, 77.
14. Rodriguez, *A Future for the Latino Church*, 61.

believes that oneness of leadership among leaders from various cultures provides this balance, or "structure," as he put it.

Leaders' communication styles are also culturally patterned. Hyun Choi explained that difficulties arose in a multicultural church because the Korean American leader used an indirect communication pattern, whereas the Anglo leader preferred direct communication.[15] Further, leaders in Western churches tend to be more event-oriented, or transactional, whereas leaders in non-Western cultures tend to be more relational.[16] Anglo leaders tend to address issues "head-on," whereas many non-Western cultures use an indirect path. Mark Branson and Juan Martínez describe a situation where the church organist was declining in ability, and the leaders from various cultures clashed on how to address the issue: "The Japanese American voices said that they should do nothing—the organist could have the job for as long as she wished. . . . But other leaders, Euro-American and Chinese American, said that it was inappropriate to allow a professional musician to continue in this situation."[17] The multicultural leadership team eventually worked out an indirect solution that blended the leadership preferences of the various cultures: An older musician (not on staff) would "have a conversation with the organist" about stepping down.[18]

Sermons Are Regularly Delivered (Thus Translated) in More Than One Language

Churches with high multiculturality require language translation if there is also high togetherness. For example, at La Casa Church in Nashville, the sermons are delivered in both Spanish and English, as one person preaches and another person consecutively translates from the stage. Over the years, the church has discovered that the "chemistry" between the preacher and interpreter is essential. It requires advance planning (especially when working in humor or wordplay) and a sense of rhythm—especially to elide the sensation of boredom

15. Choi, "Multicultural Church," 8.
16. Northouse, *Leadership*, 443.
17. Branson and Martínez, *Churches, Cultures and Leadership*, 156–58.
18. Branson and Martínez, *Churches, Cultures and Leadership*, 156–58.

while listening to an interpreter, and to avoid the impression that the sermon lasts too long.[19]

At Village Church in Beaverton, Oregon, the sermon is translated into several languages, including Spanish, Korean, and, more recently, Japanese, but is always delivered in English (otherwise they would need to hand out hundreds of translation devices to the English speakers). And the pastors of the English, Spanish, and Korean ministries share the preaching load. This way, the church is exposed to the various culturally patterned preaching styles (and hermeneutical approaches) of their leadership team.

In a fascinating study on the impact of bilingual sermons, Fikri Youssef explained that among participants in the study at La Casa Church, the preacher and translator cocreate the sermon: "Out of twenty-one valid responses, thirteen considered the interpreter at La Casa to be a co-preacher of the sermon. Seven people considered him an active partner who works with the primary preacher to deliver the sermon while only one person considered the interpreter to be a helper of the preacher. No one considered the interpreter to be merely someone who translates whatever the preacher says into another language."[20] Members said that hearing the sermon in their native language helped them connect to their cultural roots, helped clarify concepts, strengthened the impact of the message, and helped Anglos and Latinos connect to one another.[21]

Despite the benefits, there are costs to having the sermon delivered in multiple languages. While 55 percent of interviewees at La Casa Church tried to follow the sermon in both languages, 20 percent found the foreign language to be a distraction.[22] In fact, when I (Ken) described the culture-blending posture (chap. 12) to a pastor of a megachurch, he responded with a mixture of surprise and confusion: "I think it's a nice idea. . . . But, it would be hard for me to pay attention. It's hard enough for me to pay attention when it's in English, let alone a different language. So, like I said, it's a

19. Youssef, "Bilingual Preaching," 142.
20. Youssef, "Bilingual Preaching," 126.
21. Youssef, "Bilingual Preaching," 135–36.
22. Youssef, "Bilingual Preaching," 132.

beautiful picture. Sounds great, right? It's heaven on earth, heaven on earth. But . . ."

The "but" to the pastor's statement may mean "But not likely to happen here." For the vast majority of churches in the United States, the beauty of the multicultural vision in Revelation 7 is not quite powerful enough to overcome the potential obstacles. *How do some churches overcome those obstacles?* This was one of the major research questions that compelled us to write this book.

The value of hearing sermons from those of various cultural backgrounds is that pastors from cultures other than our own inevitably interpret Scripture in ways that we have not previously considered or emphasized. Martyn Snow, the bishop of Leicester—a highly intercultural area in England—uses the metaphor of a "gift exchange" to describe this confluence of hermeneutical approaches.[23] With a bit of vulnerability, the Bible reader from one cultural background bundles up all their life's experiences (shaped by their cultural and cross-cultural backgrounds) to interpret a biblical passage and offers it to the group. By offering this gift, readers from one culture enter into a relationship with members of another culture. And they each reciprocate by offering their culturally shaped interpretations of the same passage. This cross-cultural sharing of ideas helps us to all mine the Bible for all its worth.

For example, preachers of Asian backgrounds are more likely than Europeans to emphasize passages on harmony and honor;[24] interpreters from South American backgrounds may be more in tune with the role of Christianity in addressing social issues;[25] pastors of African backgrounds may emphasize the power of Christ over demons and sickness;[26] Anglo preachers are likely to emphasize the personal aspects of the atonement;[27] and believers from the Near East may emphasize biblical themes of hospitality more than those of Western European descent do.[28] The cross-cultural process of Christianity throughout

23. Snow, *An Intercultural Church.*
24. Vaughn, *Reading Romans with Eastern Eyes.*
25. Padilla, *Misión Integral.*
26. Kunhiyop, *African Christian Theology.*
27. Baker, *The Scandal of the Cross.*
28. Azumah and Babou, *Territoriality and Hospitality.*

history[29] has taken us out of our echo chambers and caused us to separate the essential aspects of Christianity from our own cultural baggage.[30]

Additionally, sermon styles vary from culture to culture. Black preaching styles are more dialogic, using "call and response." Some Black pastors described using more "whooping" and "hollering" in predominantly Black churches, and a Korean pastor described a more "passionate" preaching style in the Korean church culture.[31] Many White evangelicals prefer to take notes on three points (preferably alliterative). And while narrative preaching is popular in all cultures, certain societies far prefer storytelling over word studies and propositional truths.[32] These diverse approaches to preaching, exegesis, and applying Scripture collectively bring holistic value to a deeper understanding of God's Word.

An effective multicultural church will reflect the various cultural backgrounds not just of the preaching staff but of the congregation. Preachers must put the effort into learning how the various cultures in their congregation affect the way people interpret Scripture. Matthew Kim suggests that preachers consider what illustrations "hit home" in each of these cultures.[33] (Hint: The sermon should not always rely on baseball or football illustrations.) How do their cultures portray God? As distant? As a dictator? As a benevolent Santa Claus figure? What are the typical hopes and dreams in these cultures? Financial security? Status? Survival? Finding purpose? How can Scripture redirect or fulfill those dreams and aspirations? What modern-day idols are perpetuated in these cultures, and how does Scripture challenge those idols? What communication styles work with these cultures? Direct or indirect confrontation? Humor? Narrative? What illustrations hit home in this culture? Soccer or football? Communicators shape their message for their audience, and this can be an enriching process when the audience is highly multicultural.

29. Walls, *The Cross-Cultural Process.*
30. Nehrbass, *Advanced Missiology*, 20.
31. Edwards and Kim, *Estranged Pioneers*, 125.
32. Steffen and Armstrong, *New and Old Horizons.*
33. Kim, *Preaching with Cultural Intelligence.*

The Worship Service Represents More Than One Cultural Background Each Sunday

Multiculturality in worship is more than style. It must also take into account culturally patterned expectations for the worship service, which include the following examples:

- Time orientation, emphasis on punctuality, length of service[34]
- Use or nonuse of bulletins and other literature
- Structure in the order of the service
- Style of worship music (rhythms, instruments)
- Style of expression (dance, arts, etc.)
- Manner of greeting (hugs, handshakes, bowing, "holy kiss")
- Prayer style and language
- Language that the Scripture is read in
- Symbols used
- How the offering is made
- Presence of "altar calls"
- Use of testimonies[35]

If you have never witnessed this sort of multilingualism in church, consider the example of St. Cyprian Episcopal, a historically Black church in North Carolina. They use "a bilingual hymnal and completely bilingual worship folders so people can cross over into the 'other' language. They simultaneously recite the confession of sin, Lord's Prayer and Nicene Creed in Spanish and English. The sermon is in English, followed by a Spanish summary."[36]

First Baptist Church of Duluth, Georgia, incorporates worship styles from various cultures, such as a traditional fan dance from

34. George Yancey reports in *One Body, One Spirit* that predominantly Black services are thirty-five minutes longer than predominantly White worship services (81).

35. At Hyun Choi's All Nations United Methodist Church (a language-group posture with four ethnic-group congregations), this includes ensuring that testimonies are given by people from different ethnic backgrounds. "Multicultural Church," 9.

36. Huyser-Honig, "Four Essentials for Multicultural Worship."

South Korea to celebrate the lunar new year.[37] Similarly, the worship team at Quest Church in Seattle receives the weekly praise setlist a week in advance to prepare for the following Sunday. Included with the list are links for praise members to practice proper pronunciation of words in other languages and to become familiar with the various cultural music styles that will be incorporated in the Sunday worship.

The time of prayer can also be multilingual. At Greenford Baptist Church in West London, England, worship leaders pray in whatever language they know best. Even when congregants come forward for prayer, the person delivering the prayer may use a language other than English.[38] Worship leaders there incorporate the reggae and calypso rhythms of the Caribbean. Congregants dance in styles that represent their backgrounds. And to respect various cultural expressions related to financial giving as an act of worship, the worship leader calls people forward to touch the offering plate, even if they have already given online.[39]

During interviews, one participant shared that when her family first visited their current church, her husband began weeping when the praise team began singing in Korean. Incorporating diverse cultural rhythms, styles, and languages during worship is not just about relevance; it is often a way for individuals to draw closer to God through their heart language.

Programs and Events at the Church Represent More Than One Cultural Background

The calendar of a multicultural church reflects the rites and rituals of various cultures. Examples include the following:

- *Sabekkido* morning prayer, a "corporate prayer in the Korean custom of the Tong Sung Kido, in which everyone prays aloud simultaneously"[40]

37. Hearn, *Technicolor*, 32, 101.
38. Wise, "Multi-Ethnic Local Church," 139.
39. Wise, "Multi-Ethnic Local Church," 140–45.
40. Choi, "Multicultural Church," 10.

- Gathering for fellowship and enjoying meals with community after worship
- Celebrating various holidays, such as Cinco de Mayo, Juneteenth, and Chinese New Year[41]
- Incorporating various cultural patterns for Christian holidays and seasons like Christmas and Lent
- Programs for transferring immigrant parents' culture to their children, such as children's Saturday school programs that focus on learning other languages and traditional dances/music
- Awareness (including firsthand accounts) of significant events in other countries, and intercession for relatives there[42]

Malcolm Patten, senior pastor of Blackhorse Road Baptist Church in East London, England, describes the multicultural nature of a Christmas carol service: "I chose a few verses from each of the traditional readings and had them read in a different language by someone in the congregation. We had angels speaking in Spanish, Tamil, Yoruba, French and Polish! . . . I arranged for the English to appear on the screen while the verses in foreign languages were spoken."[43]

Multicultural programming also includes the delivery of pastoral care. People from different cultures have different expectations about how the church will interact with them when they are sick, or when there is a funeral or wedding in the family. Leadership teams must be in tune with culturally patterned values and expectations regarding these aspects of the life cycle.[44] For example, Pastor Jeff ministers in a multiethnic church with a large Hispanic constituency—some with Catholic and some with Pentecostal backgrounds. He has been asked to carry out "house blessings" to exorcise demons from every room in the house. He has had to work out how to help them feel cared for while also staying true to his own theology. He told us, "Don't let Hollywood play a factor in this. I'm not downplaying or discounting at all the satanic and demonic realm that is real and exists, but

41. George Yancey specifically mentions these three in *One Body, One Spirit*, 145.
42. Patten, *Leading a Multicultural Church*, 86.
43. Patten, *Leading a Multicultural Church*, 83.
44. Taylor, "Pastoral Care and Education."

we have authority over that, and there's no reason to give the enemy more authority in our lives for that. So I try to encourage them in that way. But sometimes those beliefs die hard."

When Mark Branson and Juan Martínez train people to deliver culturally competent pastoral care, they cover "unspoken rules regarding touching and hugging, length of visit, and the use of prayer."[45] There are also differences in how pastoral care will be delivered during a time of bereavement. Malcolm Patten explains,

> In Afro-Caribbean cultures the usual expectation is that family and friends will visit the home of the bereaved as soon as they hear of the death, whereas in others, including British culture, the bereaved may often want to be left alone. In multicultural churches embarrassment can be caused when people from Afro-Caribbean cultures turn up unannounced at a bereaved English person's home to support the person in his or her grief. On the other hand, when someone among the Afro-Caribbean community dies their relatives may wonder why none of the English people have come to support them.[46]

Additionally, multicultural programming requires discipleship materials that are not implicitly, or by default, aimed at only one of the ethnic groups in the church (whether White, Korean, Hispanic, or so on). A qualitative study on seven multiethnic churches in the Boston area revealed that participants felt that discipleship materials are "designed for middle-class, white, suburban people."[47] Therefore, "leaders of multiethnic churches must be creative and either create their own curriculum for Sunday school and their small group ministry or tweak published materials to incorporate multicultural examples to be more relevant for their population."[48]

In a multiethnic church, "the cultural interactions surround and interface with the biblical text, allowing for discipleship to occur from a multiethnic perspective. The benefit is a far richer understanding of divine truth that is less tainted by one's own cultural viewpoints."[49]

45. Branson and Martínez, *Churches, Cultures and Leadership*, 155–56.
46. Patten, *Leading a Multicultural Church*, 104.
47. Dunlow, "Disciples of All Nations," 297.
48. Nicholas, "Managing Group Conflict," 55.
49. Gushiken, "Christian Identity," 18.

CHAPTER SUMMARY

Multiculturality refers to the extent to which multiple cultures and/or languages are represented in a church's worship, sermons, and leadership styles. A church that scores high in multiculturality is typically ethnically diverse, but an ethnically diverse church does not necessarily score high in multiculturality. While ethnic diversity in a church may occur organically, multiculturality requires intentionality, planning, and buy-in from the congregation. Although this requires a great deal of effort, there are several benefits: People feel most welcome when their own cultures are represented, and members mature in their faith as they are exposed to various culturally influenced interpretations of Scripture.

Things to Watch for with Multiculturality

- Multicultural worship requires buy-in, coordination, and commitment.
- Be careful not to treat people from other cultures as tokens in an attempt to be multicultural.
- When singing worship songs in different languages, help readers with pronunciation and provide accurate translations.
- Take time to build relationships in order to create an authentic multicultural community.

REFLECTION QUESTIONS

1. What is the difference between ethnic diversity and multiculturality?
2. Why might it be difficult for some churches to have the marks of multiculturality described in this chapter?
3. How have you experienced multiculturality in your community, workplace, and/or in your day-to-day activities?

For Further Reading on Multiculturality

Davis, Josh, and Nikki Lerner. *Worship Together: In Your Church as in Heaven*. Abingdon, 2015.

Downie, Jonathan. *Multilingual Church: Strategies for Making Disciples in All Languages*. William Carey, 2024.

Hearn, Mark. *Technicolor: Inspiring Your Church to Embrace Multicultural Ministry*. B&H, 2017.

Kim, Matthew. *Preaching with Cultural Intelligence: Understanding the People Who Hear Our Sermons*. Baker Academic, 2017.

Rah, Soong-Chan. *Many Colors: Cultural Intelligence for a Changing Church*. Moody, 2010.

Snow, Martyn. *An Intercultural Church for a Multicultural World: Reflections on Gift Exchange*. Church House, 2024.

Van Opstal, Sandra. *The Next Worship: Glorifying God in a Diverse World*. InterVarsity, 2016.

CHAPTER 2

Oneness

> Complete my joy by being of the same mind, having the same love, being in full accord and of one mind.
>
> —Philippians 2:2

Chapter Goals

By the end of this chapter, you should be able to do the following:

- identify marks of oneness
- evaluate the advantages and disadvantages of oneness in structure for a multisite, multicongregation church
- reflect on the level of oneness in your own congregation

Are the finances, leadership team, vision, growth plan, and communication channels shared by all congregations and sites that make up your church? Oneness refers to the extent to which the church structures (finances, procedures and rules, and vision) are shared by all those who meet on campus. Most churches are high in oneness, even if they have multiple services or even multiple locations. However, some, like those with a shared-space posture (chap. 6), do not have a single budget, leadership team, brand, or vision. They are low in oneness. Note that as we use the term "oneness" here, it does not refer to the theological sense that Christians are all one in Christ (1 Cor. 12:12–13; Gal. 3:28), nor to the concept that we share one common ancestor in Adam (Acts 17:26). And oneness here does not refer to the extent that people in the church feel connected to one another, as important as that is (Rom. 12:15; 1 Cor. 12:26). These are important biblical concepts, but we are interested in a very specific type of oneness when it comes to measuring a church's cross-cultural posture. A fascinating study of oneness by the Leadership Network revealed that a shared vision is the primary factor that contributes to oneness, followed by a single leadership structure, a single church name, a shared preaching/teaching content, a shared worship style, and lastly, a shared budget.[1]

Even multisite or "multicongregation" churches that meet at different locations can have high oneness if they have "a common vision, budget, leadership, and board."[2] These multisite or multicongregations can be either monocultural or multicultural. For instance, the language-group posture, described in chapter 10, has high multiculturality and high oneness but low togetherness. Yet when Lyle Schaller first developed a taxonomy of multisite churches, he did not envision that one reason for having a single church structure (or high oneness) with multiple congregations would be the complexity of reaching people from various languages in the community.[3] Three decades after Schaller's study, the language-group posture is a common one for churches.

Gerardo Martí's study focuses on churches that have "at least two distinct ethnic groups sharing a common congregational life and governance."[4] This highlights oneness, but our study of various multicultural churches in the United States has demonstrated a need to be more precise in terminology. We began to realize that oneness

1. Surratt, Ligon, and Bird, *The Multi-Site Church Revolution*, 130.
2. Surratt, Ligon, and Bird, *The Multi-Site Church Revolution*, 18.
3. Schaller, *Innovations in Ministry*.
4. Martí, "Mosaic on Mission," 19.

and togetherness are not the same. As we show in part 2, some church postures have a single leadership structure with at least two distinct ethnic groups, but the groups do not worship together (this would be the language-group posture in chap. 10). And some churches have two or more distinct ethnic groups with shared governance but have a single worship style (both the multiethnic posture in chap. 9 and the reconciling posture in chap. 11 fit this description).

Some would argue that it is impossible for a multisite or multicongregation to have oneness if people do not worship together.[5] Is such an organization even technically a church (because *ekklēsia*, after all, refers to those assembled)? Those who do not attend or lead multicultural congregations may especially take issue—on theological or ideological grounds—with a church's decision to separate the budgets, leadership team, and branding among the various congregations under its purview.

Below we explore the five marks of oneness.

One Leadership Team (Pastors, Staff, and Elders) over All Ethnic/ Cultural Groups in the Church

In multisite or multicongregation models, high oneness involves the existence of one set of elders and pastors for all congregations or sites that are part of the church—though the actual worship leaders and preachers may be site-specific, depending on the various services and ethnic campuses. In contrast, a single site may have low oneness if various ethnolinguistic congregations share the site, but do not share a vision, brand, budget, or leadership team.

Oneness within the leadership team allows for each leader to develop their own gifts and specializations because there are other members on the team who have complementary skills. Additionally, because oneness requires plurality and transparency, it has the benefit of a high level of accountability. High oneness is also efficient: It allows the leadership team to combine resources; it eliminates the need to reinvent the wheel at each campus.[6]

5. Hammett, "Multi-Site Church."
6. Surratt, Ligon, and Bird, *The Multi-Site Church Revolution*, 47, 51.

A fascinating example of high oneness with low togetherness across congregations is the partnership between a predominantly White church, Hope Presbyterian, and a predominantly Black church, Bethel New Life. They began sharing a church campus in Wheaton, Illinois, and now they share the same pastor: Ron Beauchamp.[7] In this case, the high oneness and low togetherness is not due to language or geographic differences. Instead, it is due to historical trajectories of the two ethnically different congregations that are trying to reach a higher level of cooperation.

But most scenarios with high oneness and low togetherness are due to language differences. For example, Manuel Ortiz explains that First Baptist Church of Flushing, New York, fits the description of a church with high oneness, even though there are several congregations within the church, based on ethnolinguistic differences. "The church considers itself one church with different language groups. The staff works together as a team rather than as independent groups making their own decisions."[8]

High oneness is also reflected in a church's eldership. Keith Watkins describes the process whereby four ethnolinguistic congregations at First Church of the Nazarene in Los Angeles are governed by a single elder board: "The number of representatives for each congregation is determined annually by a formula that includes each congregation's income, average attendance and total membership."[9]

Note a concern about oneness in multisite or multicongregation approaches: Oneness can result in low autonomy on the part of the various congregations. Picture a scenario where a prominent lead pastor at a large congregational site exerts a heavy influence over ethnic minority congregations that fall under the church's purview.

One Budget for All Campuses or Congregations

Of course, in single-site churches oneness in budgeting makes sense. It's hard to imagine a single-site church with a single congregation

7. Lindsay, "Two Churches, Two Races, One Pastor."
8. Ortiz, *One New People*, 79.
9. Watkins, "Multi-Language Congregations," 135.

operating on several budgets! On the other end of the spectrum, in arrangements where ethnic minority congregations rent the space of a more established church, budgets may be entirely separate.

In multisite churches (whether monolingual or those with various language services) the budgeting is more complex. There are some advantages for multisite congregations to pool resources (i.e., to have a high degree of oneness in budgeting). Rick Dunn uses terminology from the business world to describe the advantage of such oneness: "A well implemented multi-site strategy can lead to economies of scale and free up financial resources for Kingdom impact. For example, a typical church of 2,000 people would normally require a staff of 20–30 people. A multi-site church of the same size would only need a staff of 8–10 people. This is made possible through the Central Team that serve[s] the administrative needs of multiple campus[es,] creating the economies of scale."[10]

What percent of the budget is the church willing to commit toward a separate congregation? And for how long will they provide support at that level? Geoff Surratt, Greg Ligon, and Warren Bird's study of multisite churches revealed that the typical mother church contributed 5 to 10 percent of its budget to the sponsored congregation, and expected the congregation to become self-sufficient within a year.[11] The culture of multisite churches may have changed since this study was carried out, and expectations may be different for mother churches that support church plants in immigrant communities. But a church's commitment level to each of the five MOTIVEs will impact both the top dollar amount they are willing to contribute to make these congregations successful and the degree to which they expect the various congregations to achieve self-sufficiency.

Oneness in budgeting can be a radical form of generosity and advocacy for churches that have a language-group posture. In this scenario, wealthier established congregations say, "We got you. We have your back," to members of a fledgling immigrant congregation. Such oneness in the budget is more than sponsorship; it's a commitment inspired by Acts 2:44 to have "had all things in common"

10. Dunn, "A 'New' Vision for Multi-Sites."
11. Surratt, Ligon, and Bird, *The Multi-Site Church Revolution*, 104–5.

and in Galatians 6:2 to "bear one another's burdens." Imagine a multicultural church where wealthier families contribute gifts to the church that are used to provide resources (including scholarships for school and help with housing to lower-income families).[12] Clarkston International Bible Church is an example. The church pools resources to provide furniture, clothing, and food to the newly arrived immigrants in their church.[13]

Mason Keiji Okubo, pastor of Immanuel First Lutheran Church in West Covina, California, described his church's partnership with a Vietnamese congregation. The budgets are not shared, but the Anglo congregation discovered a ministry opportunity as they participated in a fundraiser. "A few years ago, we had a joint fundraiser to raise money for a project for the Vietnamese congregation. . . . When we did this joint fundraiser, it was the first time that many of the English-speaking members of Immanuel had worked closely with the Vietnamese members. They totally enjoyed it. In fact, in working together, many have come to develop friendships with each other."[14]

However, oneness in budgeting also raises problems for multisite or multicongregation models. Thomas White and Jon Mark Yeats are concerned that high oneness in budgeting robs local congregations of autonomy. "Offerings taken at the satellite campus are deposited into the main campus's accounts, and the bean counters there determine how much goes back out to meet the needs of the satellite. While this is efficient and provides for cost sharing, the ramifications are huge. Your local congregation has zero control."[15]

Additionally, Geoff Chang, pastor of Wornall Road Baptist Church in Kansas City, Missouri, recognizes that many fledgling "immigrant congregations" rely on a "unified budget in which giving and expenses from every congregation are lumped together."[16] But he warns that such pooling may fail to recognize significant increases in the financial health of minority congregations. "While this avoids some difficulties, it unfortunately hides the growth and contribution of each

12. Williams and Jones, *In Church as It Is in Heaven*, 84.
13. Byrd, *The Multiethnic, Multicongregational Church*, 142.
14. Okubo, "Unity and Diversity," 205.
15. White and Yeats, *Franchising McChurch*, 81–82.
16. Chang, "Reflections on 'One Assembly.'"

congregation. It robs the congregations of the opportunity to relate to one another in humility and gratitude. It also makes it more difficult for members to take responsibility for supporting those who teach them the Word (Gal. 6:6; 1 Tim. 5:17–18)."[17]

A large church in California has a substantial English congregation and a smaller, but growing, Spanish congregation, as well as a ministry to the deaf. The lead pastor explained that the pastors of the ministry to the deaf and the Spanish congregation have both echoed a desire for the amount of the offerings given by the various congregations to be noted, in hopes that the amount given by the ministry to the deaf and the Spanish congregation can justify hiring additional staff in these ministries. The senior pastor told me (Ken) how he responded to this request from the pastor of the Spanish ministry: "I told him, 'Well, if, for some reason, they're not tithing as much, the answer is not no. The answer is, "We just have to treat this ministry like all other departments as we think through, what does the church absolutely need right now?"'"

Because of the push and pull with this issue, churches need to determine their commitment level to oneness. If they are not highly committed to oneness, they must have a long-term plan for transitioning from dependence to independence.[18]

One Vision Held by All Ethnic/Cultural Groups and Congregations in the Church

Churches are built around a vision, so a church does not have high oneness unless all of its sites and congregations share a single vision and purpose. We address the importance of inclusionary vision in chapter 4, but here we think through how various church postures have different degrees of a shared overall ministry vision.

In scenarios where a congregation rents space from a more established church, there is low oneness of ministry vision. This is a fundamental difference between the shared-space posture and the language-group posture. Both have low togetherness, but in the

17. Chang, "Reflections on 'One Assembly.'"
18. ChurchSalary, "How Multisite Churches Pay Campus Pastors."

language-group posture a single leadership team is held together by a shared ministry vision. For example, The Grove Community Church in Riverside, California, has an English congregation and a Spanish congregation. Pastor Fabian, who leads The Grove Español, explained to me (Ken) that The Grove has "one vision across the congregations: 'Being changed by God to reach the world.'" We asked Daniel Bishop, lead pastor at The Grove, why oneness of vision among the two congregations is important. His answer was rooted in an important leadership principle: Any organization—but especially nonprofits—needs to be ruthlessly driven by their mission.[19] He explained that *all* ministries of the church—whether children's ministry or the ministry to the deaf, or the coffee shop—share the vision of the church. Therefore, it is perfectly reasonable that the Spanish congregation would share this vision as well. Pastor Daniel added that the oneness is about aligning not with the senior pastor but with the vision of the church. He said, "Our Spanish pastor told me, 'Daniel, I want to make sure that I'm on the same page as you.' And I said, 'I don't want you to be on the same page as me, I want you to be on the same page as the church.'"

If your church has a shared-space posture, you may consider how the churches would benefit from a more shared vision.

One Growth Plan, Including Sermon Series and Membership Process for All Ethnic/Cultural Groups and Congregations in the Church

Oneness also involves a shared scope and sequence for membership classes, discipleship, and sermon series. Churches with a high degree of oneness but a low degree of togetherness (i.e., the multisite or multicongregation churches) have various approaches toward the oneness of the sermon series:

- **The campus pastor approach:** Pastors preach at their respective sites but are under a single organizational chart. Note that campus pastors may engage in a high degree of collaboration as they create their messages, thus creating oneness in the growth plan.

19. Barna, *The Power of Vision*.

- **The video venue approach:**[20] When congregations prefer to hear from a well-known pastor, they watch a video or simulcast of the sermon. In cases where the church service is in more than one language, the sermon is translated.
- **The rotation approach:** A team of pastors rotates among the campuses, sharing the preaching responsibilities.
- **The cross-cultural approach:** In multilingual churches, campus pastors preach in the languages spoken by the people at their respective campuses. For example, Mariners Church in Irvine, California, has a Spanish-speaking site where the campus pastor preaches in Spanish. Such oneness obviously requires a tremendous amount of planning for multilingual churches. Pastor Daniel Bishop, at The Grove, explains how they achieve oneness:

> Even our sermons that we plan out, we have a meeting on Tuesdays, of which our deaf pastor is there, and our Spanish pastors are there, and we're brainstorming the sermon together in the text that we're going to study. So it's not just a matter of, "Here's what I'm teaching, and you all say the exact same thing." It's more, "Here's the text, and what do we all think? And can we learn together?" So that's important. And our youth pastors are there. Everyone who teaches the sermon is there, and everyone in the whole staff is invited to come to that. We even have laypeople come if they'd like to come.

A member of the Spanish congregation at a church with a language-group posture explained that such oneness leads to difficulties in translation: "This is the first time that I think the English congregation has actually seen what a Spanish church looks like. . . . So we have to consider the communication part of things. They'll say, 'We're going to call the sermon series Boldness.' And when it comes to Spanish, there's no literal translation for that. So we have to do research. We said *viviendo sin límites* [living without limits]."

20. Easum and Travis, *Beyond the Box*.

Regardless of the difficulties, oneness helps hold the Spanish and English ministries together at The Grove. Pastor Daniel told us, "For first-generation people who don't know a lot of English, or they don't know any at all, they typically have family members that do, and they want to go to church together. We see this a lot. Their kids, who are adults, are going to the English-speaking service, and the grandparents are sitting in the Spanish service, and they're all hearing the exact same message."

One Major Communication Channel Going to All Ethnic/Language Groups

Oneness also involves a single brand. This includes the name and logo of the church and all communication channels. For example,

- Is there a single website?
- Are emails sent to all congregations/sites, or are they site-specific?
- Is there a single church blog?
- Is there a single membership database?
- Are church meetings carried out together—perhaps by teleconference?[21]

CHAPTER SUMMARY

Churches' cross-cultural postures are in part determined by their degree of oneness. Churches with multiple sites or separate congregations (due to language differences) have a strong case for maintaining oneness of the leadership team, vision, budget, and growth plans across the various sites or congregations. This oneness helps the church to relentlessly pursue its mission, and it helps foster cohesion across the various ethnolinguistic groups.[22] However, oneness does present a danger: The voices of the more dominant leader and

21. Surratt, Ligon, and Bird, *The Multi-Site Church Revolution*, 139–40.
22. House and Allison, *MultiChurch*.

congregation might be prioritized over the needs and desires of the other sites and congregations.

Things to Watch for with Oneness

- Ensure that oneness does not create dependency.
- Ensure that oneness does not squash the voice of the minority congregations.
- Ensure that oneness does not result in uniformity but rather focuses on embracing differences while maintaining shared purpose.

REFLECTION QUESTIONS

1. What are the advantages of extending a high degree of oneness over multiple congregations and sites?
2. What are the disadvantages of extending a high degree of oneness over multiple congregations and sites?
3. If a multicongregation or multisite church has high oneness, how can it ensure that the voices of the desires and needs of the various language groups or campuses are being addressed?

For Further Reading on Oneness

Harrison, Rodney, Tom Cheyney, and Don Overstreet. *Spin-Off Churches: How One Church Successfully Plants Another*. B&H Academic, 2008.

House, Brad, and Gregg Allison. *MultiChurch: Exploring the Future of Multisite*. Zondervan, 2017.

Surratt, Geoff, Greg Ligon, and Warren Bird. *The Multi-Site Church Revolution: Being One Church in Many Locations*. Zondervan, 2006.

CHAPTER 3

Togetherness

Oh, magnify the LORD with me, and let us exalt his name together!

—Psalm 34:3

Chapter Goals

By the end of this chapter, you should be able to do the following:

- describe how togetherness is different from oneness
- identify marks of togetherness
- reflect on the level of togetherness in your own congregation

Single-site, single-congregation churches obviously have a high degree of togetherness. The congregation worships together; all children attend the same programming; small groups are composed of all the ethnic backgrounds found in the church. This level of togetherness is common not only in monocultural churches but also in multiethnic churches. Of course, for centuries in the United States, this level of togetherness was not guaranteed: Black and White people who attended the same church did not worship together. Blacks and Whites were seated separately (sometimes with dividers) and even served Communion separately.[1] Nowadays, even though the vast majority of churches (at least 75 percent of churches in the United States) tend to be monoethnic, of those that are multiethnic, the reason for low togetherness usually is language differences—or perhaps cultural differences—rather than racial segregation. (However, as we discuss below, some multiethnic, monolingual churches may have high togetherness in the pews and children's programs but still evidence low togetherness in discipleship groups or other small groups that meet in homes.)

Note that simply having multiple church services does not mean that there is low togetherness—at least not as we define it here. By togetherness, we mean that all language, cultural, and ethnic groups are together during worship services, not separate. Additionally, the children and youth programs, discipleship programs, service groups, and fellowship groups have all of the ethnic and cultural groups together rather than separate.

A lack of togetherness may seem strange or even destructive. Why wouldn't everyone in the church worship together? If people do not worship together, do they share the same church?[2] Several participants explained to us that whenever the church tried to have separate worship services (due to differences in language or worship style preferences), it caused division. But to reiterate, churches that reach various language groups often have separate services so they can reach people in a language they understand best. Thus they may have a strategic reason for low togetherness.

Scholars, leaders, and attendees recognize that there are blessings and difficulties with high togetherness when people of various ethnicities and cultures or languages worship, fellowship, and grow together.

Below, we discuss five marks of togetherness.

1. DeYoung et al., *United by Faith*, 49.
2. Leeman, "Theological Critique of Multi-Site."

All Language, Cultural, and Ethnic Groups Worship Together on Sundays

Obviously, monocultural churches (whether monoethnic or multiethnic) worship together. But this high level of togetherness is not guaranteed in churches with high multiculturality. Often, the various language groups worship separately. The exception—where there is high multiculturality and high togetherness—is a culture-blending posture (discussed in chap. 12). In this scenario, people sing in the styles and languages that represent their various cultures. The congregation may sing a song that is familiar but use a chorus or bridge in another language. Or they may sing a song that is familiar but has been translated into another language.[3] They also hear sermons in different languages (through translation).

Ian Collinge describes various approaches for implementing togetherness in worship among various cultural groups. One model is *independence*, where worship is conducted in various languages but done separately (i.e., low togetherness). In another model, *inclusion*, speakers of one language are introduced—perhaps on a rotation schedule—to songs in another language (i.e., moderate togetherness). In the *integration* model, speakers of various languages sing one another's songs (i.e., high togetherness). But Collinge goes further and describes a *collaboration*, where speakers of various languages compose new worship songs together.[4]

First Baptist Church of Duluth, Georgia, has high togetherness. On one recent Sunday, the congregation sang a multilingual adaptation of "Holy Forever,"[5] with the chorus in Mandarin, Korean, Indonesian, Thai, Burmese, and Japanese.

This sort of togetherness across the language groups takes work and cannot be rushed. Before the shared time of singing, the worship leader invited East Asian members of the church to spend nearly four minutes coaching the congregation in pronouncing "holy" in the various languages, and the total time devoted to the song was just over ten minutes.[6]

3. Davis and Lerner, *Worship Together*.
4. Collinge, "Intercultural Worship."
5. Tomlin et al., "Holy Forever."
6. First Baptist Duluth, "Sunday Worship Gathering."

But despite the hard work, congregants got the hang of it. Roy, from a multilingual church, told us, "There is one worship song where I only know the chorus in Korean because that's how we always sing it."

Laura Roberts describes how Impact Church in Washington, DC, achieved togetherness in multicultural worship:

> Each time we introduced a song in a language other than English, we explained the vision for multicultural worship and taught the new phrases to the congregation first. Planning the multilingual songs for worship sets always took significant time to find or arrange chord charts, learn and practice as a worship team, and then prepare correct slides with lyrics and translations. For these reasons, it was difficult to do more often than every few months. As our church and worship team grew more diverse, the pastor encouraged us to set an intentional goal of making it more regular.[7]

More than ten different languages are spoken by members of Bethany Church in Ellicott, Maryland. A South Asian family asked the minister of worship and arts, Sherrie McKay, to incorporate multilingualism into the praise songs. She began by having members of the Telugu language community share the significance of the translated lyrics of a familiar worship song with the worship team. Then they taught the lyrics to the congregation.[8] The congregation found such a multilingual approach awkward at first, but then, "They couldn't get that Telugu phrase out of their mind and asked when they could learn more of the song in Telugu."[9] Eventually, word got around the community that such a church existed.

Multilingual worship with high togetherness is very uncommon in the United States. It would hardly be considered "seeker sensitive" (unless the seeker happens to speak Korean, Spanish, and English!). Ironically, multicultural worship is countercultural! Sandra Van Opstal, former worship director of Urban Mission Conference, notes that multilingual worship does not align with most people's personal preferences for a worship experience—and is not even practical to pull

7. Roberts, "Diversity in Worship," A84.
8. McKay, "Multicultural Worship," 72.
9. McKay, "Episode 2."

off. Remember, "*the primary reasons we should pursue multicultural worship, however, are neither pragmatic nor trends but biblical community and mission*."[10]

Jonathan Downie observes that singing songs in other languages affirms that those languages are worthy of use in worship. "Praying in other languages demonstrates that those languages are suitable for talking to God. Giving announcements in other languages tells the congregation that those languages can communicate important information. Preaching in another language demonstrates that God speaks in other languages."[11]

Multilingual worship is about valuing the various language communities in the church body. Without the commitment to cross-cultural relationships, multilingual worship would be a mindless exercise of sounding out the syllables to a language that is unfamiliar.[12] In fact, it involves putting the interests of others above our own (Phil. 2:4). "Not every element of the service is going to be to our liking—so looking to the interests of others rather than our own is costly but necessary."[13]

Some churches—such as Church of the Nations in Minneapolis[14] and Proskuneo Ministries in Georgia—are committed to multiculturality but have such togetherness in worship only on a monthly basis, for an evening service, rather than each Sunday morning.

Translation is key to togetherness when there is high multiculturality. Some church leaders and members expressed doubt to us that people would want to go to a church regularly where the use of a translation device was required for their participation.

Children and Youth Programs Have All Cultural and Ethnic Groups Together

Monolingual churches (whether they are monoethnic or multiethnic) generally have high togetherness in their youth and children's

10. Van Opstal, *The Next Worship*, 23 (emphasis original).
11. Downie, *Multilingual Church*, 47.
12. Davis and Lerner, *Worship Together*, 30.
13. Snow, *An Intercultural Church*, 105.
14. Van Opstal, *The Next Worship*, 123.

programs. However, children's programs do not always reflect the demographics of the parents who attend. In a remarkably frank essay, Karen Eastham, the codirector of leadership development at Bridgeway Community Church in Columbia, Maryland, reflects on the cultural homogeneity of leaders in the children's ministry. Essentially, the homogeneity was endangering the church's high degree of togetherness as it marginalized families from other ethnic backgrounds. She had her leadership team audit the representation of various cultures in their promotional materials, curriculum and videos, the cultural diversity of their music, and the diversity of people onstage. They also reexamined their mission and values—even the name of the ministry.[15]

We found it difficult to get data from the various churches about how multiculturality or ethnic diversity impacts the children and youth ministries. However, one couple in a focus group from a church with a culture-blending posture mentioned that cultures in their church have different norms for how the leader handles behavioral disruptions from the youth or children: "The mother finds out that the teacher corrected a child and says, 'That's my job.' Or if the teacher says, 'Your child is tending to talk too much in class, can you help them to listen?' And the parent will say, 'Well, that's your job to correct them.'"

Additionally, a family with a Korean mother and Anglo father found that their children had a hard time participating in their predominantly Anglo youth ministry. The youth group required a greater time commitment than the parents were willing to cede to church activities. "Our kids were spending that time in music lessons, or sports practice, or working on homework." Indeed, churches with high multiculturality and high togetherness will bring out these competing cultural expectations about how (and how often) youth should spend their time at church.

Interestingly, not all churches in the United States have high togetherness in their children's ministries. Churches with the language-group and shared-space postures often have separate worship times because of language differences. Therefore, English-speaking parents arrive with their children at 9:00 a.m., whereas the Spanish-speaking

15. Eastham, "Multicultural Children's Ministry," 120.

families may arrive at 1:00 p.m. Or to flip the script a bit, consider Wilshire United Methodist, in Los Angeles, which has (homogeneous) Korean services at 8:00 a.m. and 11:45 a.m., and a multicultural English ministry for predominantly Filipino, Korean, and Latino families at 10:00 a.m. Due to the way that the language barrier separates cultural groups, the children's and youth ministries also do not have togetherness. A somewhat different model to consider is Wheaton Bible Church in West Chicago, Illinois, which offers separate children's Sunday school services for their English-speaking and Spanish-speaking congregations but has a combined youth group that meets on Wednesday evenings. The Grove, in Riverside, California, has the services in Spanish and English at the same time in separate spaces, while the children and youth (who typically are fluent in English) have high togetherness.

Discipleship Groups Are Composed of All the Language, Cultural, and Ethnic Groups

Togetherness is not just about what happens on Sundays. A high degree of togetherness means that whenever the church meets in homes and throughout the week for discipleship programs and small groups, each of these meetings represents all of the church's cultural or ethnic diversity.

It seems difficult for churches to manage the diversity in the discipleship groups. But, interestingly, East Lake Church in Irmo, South Carolina, has developed such a process. As congregants consider joining the church, they participate in a ten-week discipleship process. Even though the groups meet at the church campus, the pastor over small groups assigns participants to one of these groups based on members' home addresses. "It's not organic at all," she explained. It is planned. She keeps in mind the ethnic diversity of the group. This way, once the group has finished the ten-week process, hopefully a longer-term discipleship group has formed—one that can result in a more permanent ethnically and culturally diverse small group that meets in the neighborhood where members reside.

The exposure to diverse cultural backgrounds can deepen our understanding of discipleship. For example, Greenford Baptist

Church in West London, England, uses the Alpha course—an apologetics curriculum that is popular especially in Europe—to invite nonbelieving Asians in their community to the church. The material helped Asians "see that Christianity is not a White Religion. It also helped non-Asians appreciate the Bible from an Asian perspective."[16]

Similarly, Derwin Gray shared that small groups at Transformation Church in Indian Land, South Carolina, are purposefully multiethnic and multigenerational. "We believe that God's people mature in the faith in the context of multiethnic, multigenerational relationships. Learning from the diversity of various cultures and stages of life is essential to developing a community that can help God display the mystery of Christ."[17] Imagine what Westerners can learn from the example of those from the Majority World, who have a more biblical view about caring for the needs of aging parents![18]

A study of Mosaic Church in Los Angeles, one of the nation's largest multiethnic churches, showed that the small groups are successful at ethnic integration.

> Mosaic does not have ethnically designated small group ministries (e.g., "Asian Groups" or "Mexican American Groups") and does not target its programs to specific ethnic groups (e.g., Hispanic Ministries). Instead, participants of the study reveal a broad degree of diversity among the groups. Small groups at Mosaic are ethnically mixed; for example, groups of 8 or 12 members will routinely have as regular members at least one Caucasian, one Hispanic, and/or one Asian attender, in addition to other ethnic identities such as African American and Middle Eastern. Mosaic small group attendees are choosing to build relationships with people of different ethnicities since within the structure of Mosaic, the choice of life group is left to the individual.[19]

One member of a highly multicultural church in our study said that she values multicultural Bible study because she is exposed to interpretations she had not previously considered. For example, she learned from the Asian person in her study group that in the phrase

16. Wise, "Multi-Ethnic Local Church," 48.
17. Gray, *Building a Multiethnic Church*, 180.
18. Parrett, "Culturally Sensitive Minister," 140.
19. Martí, "Mosaic on Mission," 22.

"your body is a temple" (1 Cor. 6:19), "your" is plural and can refer to the collective body of the church, not to an individual's body.

The best "proof" for how this high level of togetherness can be beneficial for the church is the reality that many Christians from Africa, Asia, South America, and Oceania hold a high view of Scripture, whereas Americans and European churchgoers are increasingly less likely to trust what the Bible says. Timothy Tennent insists, "While Western churches are looking increasingly like either entertainment centers or politically correct corporations, the African church is busy preaching the gospel of Jesus Christ, baptizing new believers, and planting churches. . . . Therefore, we must learn to stand shoulder to shoulder with our African brothers and sisters, who are in the bright sunrise of a great movement of God across the continent of Africa, and allow them to teach us and help us to bring renewal and revitalization back to the Western church."[20]

An interesting flip side to this cultural sharing is that while African Christians who move to the West are likely to remain religiously devout, they report being heavily influenced by Western podcasts, books, and culture—often with interpretations more liberal than those held by their relatives in Africa.[21]

As these examples demonstrate, having diverse linguistic, ethnic, and cultural perspectives in gatherings—whether while reading and studying Scripture or in small group discussions—provides an opportunity to deepen our understanding of what it means to be disciples of Jesus.

Fellowship Events Throughout the Year Are for All Language, Cultural, and Ethnic Groups Together

Just as high togetherness means that *discipleship* happens together, it also means that *fellowship* represents all the ethnic, language, and cultural groups in the church. The first thing that comes to mind, of course, is the potluck after worship. Do all language and cultural groups eat together whenever there is a potluck (high togetherness),

20. Tennent, *World Christianity*, 105–6.
21. Ola, "African Millennial Christians."

or only on special occasions (lower togetherness)? To take another example, despite having three separate sites, Madison Square Christian Reformed Church in Grand Rapids, Michigan, hosts joint fellowship gatherings and fitness classes for all members, regardless of which congregation they attend.[22]

The Grove has a language-group posture, so there is lower togetherness (due to language differences) but high oneness. The leaders are intentional in continuing to bring the Spanish-speaking and English-speaking members together for events like the Christmas service and Mother's Day. Andrea, a member of the Spanish-speaking congregation, recalled that at the last Christmas service, "We had familiar faces as greeters, people who were just at the door so they could recognize them" and give them a translation device. Sixty devices were handed out, but it looks like several hundred will be needed next year. This level of togetherness sent a powerful message. "A lot of the feedback that we got was 'We felt like we were part of the church just seeing our folks up on stage being a part of something as big as our Christmas production.'"

One fascinating reason why multicongregation churches may choose to have low togetherness is that congregations from certain cultural backgrounds prefer to meet together far more frequently than those from other backgrounds.[23] For example, at Village Church in Beaverton, Oregon, all peoples of varying ethnicities worship together during the Sunday service, but some of their "DNA Groups" are low in togetherness and instead have fellowship groups along ethnic lines, due to culturally patterned expectations (and differences in the meals prepared). The DNA Groups include gatherings for the Korean, Hispanic, Japanese, Hindi, and African American / Black affinity groups.

Service and Outreach Programs Are Composed of All the Language, Cultural, and Ethnic Groups in the Church

Despite ethnic and linguistic differences, some churches have collaborated across cultural and ethnic boundaries to better serve the needs

22. Koo, *From an Ethnic to a Multicultural Church*.
23. Ortiz, *One New People*, 65.

of the surrounding community. For instance, members of Mosaic Church in Little Rock, Arkansas, reached out to their community by "going door-to-door in order to meet the neighbors and identify needs. Given the demographic make-up of this small community, their teams included both English and Spanish speakers of varying ethnic backgrounds."[24]

In his study of Madison Square Christian Reformed Church, a multiethnic, multisite church in Grand Rapids, Michigan, Byoung Ok Koo reported that when the church began reaching out to the neighborhood, they tried to meet the "felt needs" of the community by providing a food pantry, counseling, education in financial management, parenting classes, and even fixing and giving away cars.[25] And this in turn brought more people of various ethnic backgrounds to their church. "When a church serves its neighbors regardless of their ethnic/racial backgrounds, it helps the congregation to open their arms and have a passion for diverse people."[26]

Likewise, Gerardo Martí discovered that the service projects at Mosaic Los Angeles fostered friendships across ethnicities. Congregants told him that they made friends with others in the church as they went on short trips to Mexico and when they worked on a theater production to reach out to the community.[27]

CHAPTER SUMMARY

Whereas oneness refers to a single vision, leadership structure, and discipleship plan, togetherness refers to the extent to which the various ethnolinguistic groups in the church worship, fellowship, and serve together. Just as there are multiple explanations for high or low oneness, there are legitimate reasons why a church may have high or low levels of togetherness. For example, a multiethnic church may not need separate services if the entire congregation, despite being ethnically diverse, predominantly speaks one language and shares a

24. DeYmaz, *Building a Healthy Multi-Ethnic Church*, 123.
25. Koo, *From an Ethnic to a Multicultural Church*, 162.
26. Koo, *From an Ethnic to a Multicultural Church*, 162.
27. Martí, "Mosaic on Mission," 221.

preferred worship style. A church that serves one or more immigrant communities may opt for low togetherness due to language differences (and the awkwardness of simultaneous translation). Lastly, some take the bold step to have high togetherness by combining all language groups in a multilingual service.

Things to Watch for with Togetherness

- Avoid tokenism (even when introducing worship songs in other languages and styles).
- Ensure that high togetherness is not another form of assimilation.
- Make sure you are meeting the needs of the various cultural groups.

REFLECTION QUESTIONS

1. What are the benefits of having various language and culture groups worship and grow together?
2. Why might one church prefer a high degree of togetherness whereas another church may prefer a low level of togetherness?
3. If your church has low togetherness, how can you encourage more togetherness?

For Further Reading on Togetherness

Anderson, David, and Margarita Cabellon, eds. *Multicultural Ministry Handbook: Connecting Creatively to a Diverse World.* InterVarsity, 2010.

CHAPTER 4

Inclusionary Vision

Learn to do good; seek justice, correct oppression; bring justice to the fatherless, plead the widow's cause.

—Isaiah 1:17

Chapter Goals

By the end of this chapter, you should be able to do the following:

- identify marks of inclusionary vision
- evaluate your own church's inclusionary vision

Some churches become multiethnic organically but not intentionally. There is something attractive about this sort of "accidental diversity." In fact, in a climate that is suspicious of terms like "multiculturalism" and "diversity, equity, inclusion," some church leaders and members are intentionally unintentional (i.e., colorblind) about any degree of ethnic diversity in their church. A White pastor of a megachurch in Atlanta (that happens to have a multiethnic posture) brushed aside our book idea. He told us, "Here we teach people that there is only one race, the human race."

The colorblind approach may cause churches to miss out on the *value* of different perspectives and experiences. And it may lead to churches that are technically ethnically diverse but do not have high levels of cohesion. Sarah Shin explains that the solution to building relationships with people of different ethnic backgrounds is not to be colorblind; rather, it is to build "ethnicity-aware trust."[1] "Intentionality is important because the social tendencies in the United States lean toward racial separation instead of integration. . . . It is important that the clergy and laity of the church are consistently in active conversation about how they can create and maintain their multiracial makeup."[2]

Inclusionary vision "begins with the end in view. It attempts to overcome, exceed, and transcend the limits imposed by race, culture, class, and language."[3] The congregation can be diverse but still not have meaningful cross-ethnic or cross-cultural relationships unless there are "structures in the church that allow people of different races to meet together and get to know one another across racial groups."[4] Mark DeYmaz, from the Mosaix Global Network, describes the role of vision in addressing racial issues: "[It] is my sincere hope and belief that the emerging movement to establish multi-ethnic churches throughout the United States and beyond will have the effect of dismantling institutional racism within the local church through the application of long-forsaken New Testament teaching concerning its very nature and calling."[5]

Although Little Rock is a diverse city, Sundays often remain a highly segregated time. As a result, multiethnic churches like Mosaic Church of Central Arkansas must be intentionally inclusive to bring people of different backgrounds together. But Mosaic isn't just multiethnic; it's also socioeconomically diverse. From the beginning, Pastor Mark envisioned a church that reflected diversity not only in

1. Shin, *Beyond Colorblind*, 103.
2. DeYoung et al., *United by Faith*, 178.
3. Choi, "Multicultural Church," 93.
4. DeYoung et al., *United by Faith*, 178.
5. DeYmaz, *Building a Healthy Multi-Ethnic Church*, 35.

race and ethnicity but also in income and social status. This commitment to community was evident in Mosaic's partnerships with several local organizations. These include a gym, a food bank that provides weekly meals along with shower and laundry services, a medical clinic, and a counseling center.

Inclusionary vision can increase the other four MOTIVEs. For example, one way that churches can grow in multiculturality is to make sure that multiple voices are present at the table. At Quest Church in Seattle, leaders and members are intentional about recognizing voices that might be missing from the discussion. One church member shared with us, "One of the things Quest is really good at is always asking, 'Who's not at the table yet? Whose voice are we not hearing from yet?' And then when that's identified, we bring them in." When we further asked how their church is able to ask minoritized people for their participation without making them feel like "tokens," a member of the church, Jessie, explained that there is a culture of "invitation without expectation," meaning that church leaders may approach underrepresented members with an invitation for representation by saying something like, "Hey, we see this and we feel like this voice is missing. Would you consider it, or do you know someone else who could bring this voice to our decision-making?"

Additionally, while ethnic diversity can be unplanned, multicultural worship cannot be achieved without intentionality. Multiculturality does not "just happen; there must be intentionality in a church's plans to grow as a multicultural church."[6] Churches do not discover at some point that somehow their worship songs are in various languages and their programming is addressing issues of racial or ethnic inclusion! As we will show in chapter 12 (on the culture-blending posture), multiculturality in the worship service is hard work. The congregation needs to "buy in" to the vision. Byoung Ok Koo's study of Korean churches discovered that intentionality on the part of the immigrant Korean leadership was essential for the church's transition from monocultural (Korean) to multicultural.[7] As Mark DeYmaz

6. Lewis-Giggetts, *The Integrated Church*, 140.
7. Koo, "Multicultural Congregations."

and Harry Li explain, "While it is true that a multi-ethnic church is a work of God, it does not just happen. You must take intentional steps to turn the vision into reality. . . . Intentionality, then, is both an attitude and an action. It must permeate and inform every corridor of a multi-ethnic church."[8]

Just as the multiethnic posture happens organically, without an overt inclusionary vision, the shared-space posture is highly multicultural without a high degree of planning or buy-in from the congregation. In this posture, churches that rent out their campus in the afternoons to a congregation of a different ethnic group may discover that multiple languages, celebrations, foods, and worship styles are now on campus. And at times, the multiculturality may "bleed over" into the host congregation. For example, members of the Anglo congregation at The Fount, in Fountain Valley, California, were pleased to see the sanctuary decorated for Tet (Vietnamese New Year). But in the shared-space posture, multiculturality is a by-product of sharing space; it is not intentionally built into the DNA of the church.

Countless churches have a vision for reaching "all people" or even reaching "the nations," and as lofty (and biblical) as that vision is, it is aspirational but not self-reflective on how the church will "create and maintain an integrated congregation."[9] It is true that a common vision such as "glorifying God and reaching the nations" can create unity across ethnic lines, but such a vision alone does not provide a road map for how relationships within the church will be interethnic and multicultural. Therefore, inclusionary vision here refers to the degree to which a church embodies a specific vision of becoming multicultural and/or multiethnic. Does its programming reflect efforts to achieve that vision? Does the leadership structure facilitate that vision? Does the congregation support that goal?

Inclusionary vision requires study. Leadership teams at churches need to devote time to learning about their surrounding community and to developing strategies for inclusion (in partnership with the various demographics in their community). When leaders of

8. DeYmaz and Li, *Leading a Healthy Multi-Ethnic Church*, 45.
9. Yancey, *One Body, One Spirit*, 109.

Greenford Baptist Church in West London, England, discerned that it was becoming more ethnically diverse, they sent their pastor on a four-month sabbatical to study multicultural churches. Subsequently, the church leadership team educated itself on multiculturality.[10]

A number of cases have been made for *why* a church should be intentional about its inclusiveness of the ethnicities and cultures in its town or city:

- **The Trinity:** The Father, Son, and Spirit model a relationship of diversity and perfect unity.[11]
- **The Great Commission:** We are commanded to reach people of all *ethnē* (Matt. 28:19–20).
- **The example of Jesus and the early church in the book of Acts:** Jesus reached across ethnic and cultural lines, and the story of the early church is a cross-cultural one.
- **Relevance:** The world is becoming more multicultural, mixed-race, and inclusive, and if your church doesn't get on board, it will be seen increasingly as irrelevant. George Yancey found that multiracial churches are growing at a faster rate than mono-racial ones.[12]
- **Diverse gifts:** We are stretched and blessed as we are exposed to the various values and perspectives of people who come from backgrounds other than our own (1 Cor. 12).
- **Testimony:** A blended church demonstrates an "out of this world" level of reconciliation (see John 17:21).[13]
- **Urgency:** Racial tensions divide us and disproportionately affect ethnic minorities. Racially based injustices don't go away on their own. The church has a prophetic responsibility to be engaged in justice.[14]

Below, we discuss five marks of inclusionary vision.

10. Wise, "Multi-Ethnic Local Church."
11. Kwiyani, *Multicultural Kingdom*, 95.
12. Yancey, *One Body, One Spirit*, 35.
13. DeYoung et al., *United by Faith*, 184–86.
14. Perkins, *One Blood*.

Inclusion of Various Races and Ethnicities Is Expressly Part of This Specific Church's Vision or Mission Statement

Some churches have multiculturality or racial/ethnic unity built into their mission statements. Some examples include:

- **Bridgeway Community Church in Columbia, Maryland:** "Our vision is to be a multicultural body of fully devoted followers of Christ moving forward in unity and love to reach our community, our culture and our world for Jesus Christ."[15]
- **Christ Central Church in Charlotte, North Carolina:** "Christ Central Church seeks to be a racially diverse church community."[16]
- **MacArthur Blvd Baptist Church in Irving, Texas:** "We want to be generationally, culturally, ethnically, and socio-economically diverse. Why? Because the kingdom of God is intentionally diverse—God is intentionally redeeming a people for Himself from every nation on earth—and we are to be a reflection of His kingdom."[17]
- **Trinity Lutheran Church in Portland, Oregon:** "Trinity is a diverse, vibrant community of forgiven sinners sharing the unconditional love of Jesus with all."[18]
- **New Community Church in Sidcup, England:** "We are a diverse, inter-generational, Bible-believing, Holy Spirit–led community of people from all walks of life, on a mission to make Jesus known to our local communities, and to the nations of the world."[19]
- **Grace Church in Rochester, New York:** "Grace Church is a diverse, growing family of Christian believers who celebrate God's

15. Bridgeway Community Church, "Mission and Vision," accessed February 7, 2026, https://www.bridgeway.cc/about-us/.

16. Christ Central Church, "Our Vision," accessed February 7, 2026, http://christcentralchurch.com.

17. MacArthur Blvd Baptist Church, "Our Vision," accessed February 7, 2026, https://macarthurblvd.org.

18. Trinity Lutheran Church, "Mission Statement," accessed February 7, 2026, https://trinitylutheranportland.org.

19. New Community Church, "Our Vision, Mission, and Values," accessed February 7, 2026, https://newcom.church/discover-more/our-vision-mission-and-values.

grace and proclaim the message of Jesus Christ in word and deed to the communities of greater Rochester and around the world."[20]

Some churches go beyond a mission statement by having position papers on racial unity or racial healing. Riverside Church in New York City published a "Black Manifesto" in 1969,[21] which it maintains on its website today.[22] Hillsong Church provides updates on how it is achieving its goals related to cultural/racial awareness of staff. This report card includes its promotion of interracial healing, and multiethnic representation in its ministries.[23]

On the other hand, First Baptist Church of Duluth, Georgia, achieved a culture-blending posture, and although ethnic and cultural diversity were part of the vision, they left out these specific terms in their mission statement. They chose a broader term related to unity: "We are a united community of faith that loves, reaches and disciples ALL PEOPLE for the Lord Jesus Christ."[24] The motives and measures of First Baptist Duluth, however, specifically mention inclusivity, justice, diversity, and responding to community issues.

At Quest Church in Seattle, any claim to be a place of safety and belonging for all people is impossible without actively addressing racial reconciliation. As Pastor Katey Hage, executive pastor of Quest Church, noted in an interview, "We started to have all these touch points, which made it hard to separate our conversations about race and reconciliation from the ways people have experienced oppression, injustice, or have been othered in many areas." Kaylee, a member at Quest Church whom we had the privilege of interviewing, echoed Pastor Katey's sentiment regarding reconciliation. She shared, "Reconciliation is just baked into so many different things [that we do at Quest] that it doesn't feel like its own siloed task or assignment." As a result, the church's commitment to inclusivity—especially across ethnic lines—is not just a vision but is a guiding

20. Grace Church, "Our Vision," accessed February 7, 2026, https://gracechurchpca.com.

21. Access the manifesto here: https://www.trcnyc.org/blackmanifesto/.

22. DeYoung et al., *United by Faith*, 80.

23. Hillsong, "Racial Equity."

24. Hearn, *Technicolor*, 48 (emphasis original).

principle that shapes everything they do and defines who they are. Another member of Quest, Ryker, also commented on the fact that his church is not afraid to have difficult conversations around faith and race. "We have built this tradition of having these faith and race conversations, which can be difficult. . . . The way I would put it is: if you're not down for having difficult conversations, I don't think you'll stay long at Quest."

Pastoral Staff Regularly Addresses Issues Related to Ethnic or Racial Inclusion

Obviously, it's not enough to have a mission statement. The mission must be translated into action. And leaders must take the lead on this. They must be vocal—whether in social media, or from the pulpit, or at other events and meetings.

One way that leaders address racial or cultural issues is the biblical practice of lament (Gen. 50:10; 1 Sam. 7:2; Pss. 3; 13; 22; 42; 44; 60; Isa. 1:2–20; Jer. 7:29; Lam. 2:5; Ezek. 19:14). Sandra Van Opstal described the way some churches incorporate the biblical practice of lament into their worship services. When there was a prominent incident of racially motivated violence against Blacks, the ethnically diverse congregation—composed largely of Latinos, Asians, and Blacks—lamented together.[25] Lament is a biblical form of empathizing with the pain of others.

To take another example, at a rally protesting the removal of a Confederate statue in Louisville, Kentucky, a demonstrator held a sign that read, "Diversity equals white genocide." The next day, Pastor Timothy Paul Jones led his multiracial church in a time of lament for the sinful racist attitudes in the town.[26] Lament involves a public acknowledgment of a hurtful act.

Some churches are so intentional about the role of their leadership in racial and cultural issues that they create staff positions like "Pastor of Inclusion" or have worship facilitators who are specifically tasked "to integrate and develop multicultural prayer and worship."[27]

25. Van Opstal, *The Next Worship*, 71.
26. Williams and Jones, *In Church as It Is in Heaven*, 34.
27. Wise, "Multi-Ethnic Local Church," 140.

The Church Has Programming to Address Ethnic or Racial Inclusion

But it's not enough for the leaders alone to take a stand on ethnic/racial inclusion. Such a vision must be built into the programming of the church. Curtiss Paul DeYoung and his coauthors describe the efforts of Park Avenue United Methodist Church in Minneapolis, Minnesota. The church brought in musicians and Christian activists such as Tony Campolo and John Perkins. They also added to their programming musical performances from people of different cultural backgrounds—thus including the various ethnic groups in their community.[28]

Other ways to build programming related to cultural and racial unity include:

- Activism: marching, protesting, organizing, boycotting
- Awareness campaigns
- Voter mobilization
- Community events incorporating various racial/ethnic groups

Efrem Smith, co-lead senior pastor of Midtown Church in Sacramento, describes his church's involvement in issues related to racial unity in 2020.

> Yes, we made statements, but we also participated in a solidarity march with police officers, pastors and community activists. We invited speakers to our church for midweek gatherings to address the history of racial bias and systemic racism, specifically in the state of California. . . . We launched new small groups based on a book club model featuring books focused on racial reconciliation, biblical justice, and systemic bias and racism. On one hand, we dove into these issues because of our founding mission and vision. But on the other hand, we launched these initiatives based on what we were hearing from the young adults and teenagers in our church and surrounding communities.[29]

28. DeYoung et al., *United by Faith*, 92.
29. Kreiss and Smith, *Church for Everyone*, 119.

Programming for inclusion inevitably means collaborating with other churches in your area—especially across ethnoracial boundaries. Fellowship Church in Monrovia, California, has developed a think tank called Reconcile Pasadena.[30] Pastors, educators, and community leaders join a one-year cohort to study reconciliation and to form strategies for community development and activism.

Inclusionary vision may start with small steps. Centerpoint Church in Colton, California, discovered that one programming change they had to implement to respond to their community's demographics is evening services on the weekend, because many people in their target group work on Sundays. And Free Life Community Church, a culture-blending church located in an affluent suburb in Southern California, adjusts its programming because many congregants navigate heavy traffic to get there. "We are a commuter church. Our programs have to be commuter friendly as well, that's why we don't do weekly Bible studies on campus." Instead, the church hosts midweek ministries in the various neighborhoods represented by the church.

The Church Has Shaped Its Programming to Respond to Demographic Changes in the Neighborhood

George Yancey notes that one capacity required for building a multicultural church is "adaptability" to the changing needs of the community.[31] Is the community experiencing "White flight"? Has a civil war somewhere led to a rapid increase in refugees? How has the presence of a university in town changed the demographics of the community?

Amid "White flight"[32] in the 1970s and 1980s in Los Angeles, a brochure for Mosaic Church[33] read, "Many other churches are leaving the city, heading for the suburbs. They may. We will not. We're not going

30. See Reconcile Pasadena, accessed February 7, 2026, https://reconcilepasadena.squarespace.com/.

31. Yancey, *One Body, One Spirit*, 138–51.

32. Scholars have noted that flight to more ethnically (or economically) homogeneous neighborhoods is evident in all ethnic groups, but empirical research shows that Whites are slightly more likely to leave ethnically heterogeneous urban areas for more homogenous suburbs. See Pais, South, and Crowder, "White Flight Revisited."

33. At this point, the church was called "The Church on Brady."

to go. We're just going to grow."[34] The church started a food pantry and a ministry for those struggling with addiction, and it obtained a grant to start a job training program.[35] This approach not only led to strong numeric growth but also positioned Mosaic Church as one of the foremost multiethnic churches in the United States.

Churches have been highly creative in innovating responses to demographic changes in their communities. Such programs include:

- ESL classes. For example, First Baptist Church of Duluth, Georgia, operates a language institute for three hundred people.[36]
- Skills training for immigrants. For example, Clarkston International Bible Church offers job training, résumé workshops, and computer classes.[37]
- Cultural celebrations (such as Lunar New Year).
- Ministry to migrants. Village Church in Beaverton, Oregon, brings meals and toiletries to the agricultural migrant camps each summer.
- Outreach to newly arrived immigrants (including help with immigration paperwork and visas, obtaining driver's licenses, finding work, etc.).
- Culture and language classes for younger people in immigrant families (such as Korean or Vietnamese language classes, heritage dance classes, martial arts classes).
- Ministry to international students. The Grove Community Church, which is in a town with several universities, hosts a dinner for international students where congregants invite people to their homes to hear the gospel and share a meal.
- Medical clinics. Village Church has free medical clinics to help international workers process their visas and to aid immigrants in obtaining visas for family members.

34. Martí, "Mosaic on Mission," 57.
35. Martí, "Mosaic on Mission," 59.
36. Hearn, *Technicolor*, 157.
37. Byrd, *The Multiethnic, Multicongregational Church*, 144.

While churches may approach intentionality in different ways, those with a strong commitment to inclusion ensure that their programming is welcoming and representative of various ethnicities and cultural backgrounds.

People in the Church Care About Ethnic or Racial Inclusion

It didn't take long for us to realize that while it's essential for pastors to be intentional about creating an inclusive multiethnic space, the same vision and intentionality must also be shared by the congregation. During an interview, Ashley noted that for her, attending a multicultural church isn't just about the teaching; it's also about building relationships with others. "I really believe that this is what the kingdom of God looks like."

Inclusionary vision means little unless the vision is owned by the congregation. When the inclusion of diverse ethnic groups is prioritized only by those in leadership, attendees may begin to feel marginalized. For instance, during an interview, a participant mentioned that although she had attended an Asian church for over fourteen years, she was still regarded as an outsider. She said, "We are still outsiders. I recognize that if you are not Asian, you will be an outsider the rest of your life. Even if you married an Asian person or even if you can use chopsticks, you're always going to be an outsider."

On the other hand, Andrea observed the inclusionary vision that was adopted widely by members at The Grove, which has an English- and Spanish-speaking fellowship.

> I've had the opportunity to help on panels and just share my story as a daughter of immigrants, and put those realities out there. So we've experienced a lot more acceptance within our congregation, where they won't be as shy to say "hi" to Hispanics. And now there are so many Latinos there that everyone is trying to learn Spanish. Even our staff, when we went through a time where The Grove Español didn't have a pastor, the staff really, really stepped up, and they were the ones that helped me keep going with ideas, and trying to learn Spanish, and just being super supportive of our Spanish fellowship.

This inclusionary vision, which ran from the leadership through the congregation, helps Andrea feel heard and seen.

Leaders may address racial issues; they may hire diverse staff; they may build multiculturality into the worship service—but do people come to the church to experience this vision of heaven on earth? Safwat Marzouk bases this inclusionary vision on Acts 10: Peter realized that the church needed to reach across ethnic divides.[38] But it's not enough to just see the vision; you have to actually go break bread and fellowship with the Other.

David Wise interviewed forty-seven longtime members in his church to understand how they experienced the church's journey toward ethnic diversity in the congregation. For many of the White members, issues of racial disunity were theoretical and distant until an Asian member of their own church was brutally beaten by an assailant with racist motives. At that point, the issue hit home for the White members.[39] Over time, members believed that by being involved in an ethnically diverse church they were part of something bigger. They were positioning themselves against racism.[40]

The vision must be owned by members of the church if members of ethnic minority groups are going to sense that they feel welcomed. Ray Washington, lead pastor of East Lake Community Church in Irmo, South Carolina, believes that when people of color visit a majority-White church, they "watch what the majority culture does and says in church as well as in social media, before they make a decision whether that church is home and safe for them."

Church leaders are in a position to help their congregation realize the importance of owning this inclusionary vision.

CHAPTER SUMMARY

Inclusionary vision requires both intention and action. Certainly, one mark of inclusionary vision is a mission or vision statement that

38. Marzouk, *Intercultural Church*.
39. Wise, "Multi-Ethnic Local Church," 31–36.
40. Wise, "Multi-Ethnic Local Church," 158.

references the inclusion of diverse cultures or ethnic groups. However, a mission statement is not enough. An inclusionary vision drives a church to make programming decisions that include the various cultures and ethnic groups in the city or neighborhood. Additionally, while a high inclusionary vision requires buy-in from church leadership, it also demands that church members actively include others.

Things to Watch for with Inclusionary Vision

- The vision of a multiethnic, multicultural church cannot be built around the pastors or even just around the leadership team. It has to be part of the church culture.
- Work to develop cross-cultural competencies in the congregation in order to avoid misunderstandings as the church becomes more ethnically diverse.

REFLECTION QUESTIONS

1. Does your church's mission statement include the concept of cross-cultural or multiethnic interaction? Why or why not?
2. What are the concepts related to race and culture that your church is seemingly unwilling to address? Why might that be the case?
3. Is diversity "for diversity's sake" a worthwhile goal in and of itself?

For Further Reading on Inclusionary Vision

Anderson, David, and Brent Zuercher. *Letters Across the Divide: Two Friends Explore Racism, Friendship, and Faith*. Baker Books, 2001.

DeYmaz, Mark. *Building a Healthy Multi-Ethnic Church: Mandate, Commitments, and Practices of a Diverse Congregation*. Jossey-Bass, 2020.

DeYoung, Curtiss Paul, Michael O. Emerson, George Yancey, and Karen Chai Kim. *United by Faith: The Multiracial Congregation as an Answer to Race*. Oxford University Press, 2003.

Harris, Paula, and Doug Schaupp. *Being White: Finding Our Place in a Multiethnic World*. InterVarsity, 2004.

Kim, Matthew. *Preaching with Cultural Intelligence: Understanding the People Who Hear Our Sermons*. Baker Academic, 2019.

Lewis-Giggetts, Tracey M. *The Integrated Church: Authentic Multicultural Ministry*. Beacon Hill, 2011.

Mathews, Kenneth A., and M. Sydney Park. *The Post-Racial Church: A Biblical Framework for Multiethnic Reconciliation*. Kregel, 2011.

Van Opstal, Sandra. *The Next Worship: Glorifying God in a Diverse World*. InterVarsity, 2016.

CHAPTER 5

Ethnic Diversity

You shall treat the stranger who sojourns with you as the native among you, and you shall love him as yourself, for you were strangers in the land of Egypt: I am the LORD your God.

—Leviticus 19:34

Chapter Goals

By the end of this chapter, you should be able to do the following:

- identify marks of ethnic diversity in a church
- reflect on the level of ethnic diversity in your own congregation

Certainly, churches' cross-cultural postures are significantly influenced by the ethnic diversity found in the congregation. A church that is predominantly White may be less sensitized to issues of racial reconciliation than an ethnically diverse congregation. However, some predominantly White churches are visionary about racial reconciliation, but due to the lack of diversity in their congregation, they lack opportunities to foster interracial relationships within the life of the church. Or, to take another example, a church that is predominantly

Armenian will have fewer opportunities for multilingual and multicultural expressions of worship than a church that is ethnically and culturally diverse. It's the same with predominantly Korean churches, or predominantly Black churches, and so on. Churches work with the people they have in their midst, so the ethnic diversity of a congregation is a key factor that shapes a church's approach toward multicultural worship, leadership, and programming.

While the topic of ethnic diversity has become highly controversial, it is a reality that has changed national landscapes, workplaces, communities, and churches. According to the 2020 US Census, there was a significant increase in racial or ethnic diversity in the United States in the previous decade. The most recent census revealed that the "White alone, non-Hispanic" share of the population decreased from 63.7 percent in 2010 to 57.8 percent in 2020.[1] In many social settings (certain workplaces and universities), no ethnic group has a majority (i.e., over 50 percent of the population). At the start of the new millennium, multicultural church experts Curtiss Paul DeYoung, Michael Emerson, George Yancey, and Karen Chai Kim predicted that this shift would soon be reflected in churches as well: "The broad population shifts taking place in the United States are expected by the midpoint of the century to produce a country with a racial demographic that is very diverse and without a numeric majority. Such changes produce settings with an increased possibility for multiracial congregations."[2]

In 1952, Dr. Helen Kenyon (1884–1978), former moderator of the Congregational Christian Churches, referred to eleven o'clock Sunday morning—when most Protestant churches are holding services—as the "most segregated time."[3] How much progress has the church made since then? How would we even measure progress? Emerson's "80 percent rule" is widely used. It states that a "multiracial congregation"

1. Jensen et al., "Two People Chosen at Random."

2. DeYoung et al., *United by Faith*, 74.

3. "Worship Hour Found Time of Segregation," *New York Times*, November 4, 1952, p. 26, col. 1. Martin Luther King Jr. made Kenyon's comment famous on *Meet the Press* on April 17, 1960. See Martin Luther King Jr., "The Most Segregated Hour in America," posted April 29, 2024, by Jason Tripp, YouTube, https://www.youtube.com/watch?v=1q881g1L_d8.

is one that has "*less than 80 percent of any single racial group.*"[4] In 1998, just 6 percent of congregations fit this criterion. Mosaix Global Network set a goal to see churches in the United States move this number to 20 percent by the year 2020, and by some measures, the dream has been realized! By 2019, 16 percent of congregations were multiracial, and because many of these multiracial churches have very large congregations, the overall percentage of people in the United States who attend a church that fits the definition of "multiracial" was at 24 percent.[5] Additionally, the denominations that are growing (evangelical and Pentecostal) are the ones that have had the greatest gains in racial diversity, so we are well on our way to seeing churches become as integrated as our workplaces and neighborhoods.

Interestingly, a high level of ethnic diversity in the congregation does not necessarily mean that the congregation or leaders will possess a high commitment to ethnic diversity. The *value* placed on inclusion was discussed in chapter 4, but certainly the *degree* of ethnic diversity is a major factor that contributes to a church's cross-cultural posture. Below, we discuss five indicators of an ethnically diverse church.

No Racial or Ethnic Group Makes Up More Than 80 Percent of the Congregation

The degree of ethnic diversity among members of the congregation is certainly the most telling metric when it comes to measuring ethnic diversity in a church. A high degree of ethnic diversity would achieve Emerson's "80 percent rule": No racial or ethnic group represents more than 80 percent of the congregation.[6] This level of diversity makes it nearly certain that interracial or intercultural relationships are common at the church.

How do congregations achieve such diversity? Emerson's study, which involved 2,500 phone interviews of interracial congregations in the United States, discovered that factors associated with ethnic diversity include "having a charismatic worship style, residing in an

4. Emerson, "A New Day" (emphasis original).
5. Dougherty et al., "Racial Diversity in U.S. Congregations," 655.
6. Emerson, *People of the Dream*, 35.

ethnically diverse neighborhood, being in an urban area, and residing in neighborhoods with higher median incomes."[7]

Note that we could not find a church in our study that actually calculates—or even collects data on—its percentage of ethnic diversity. One leadership team we interviewed had a brief discussion about whether their membership software could even collect such data, and they determined that they could create a custom field that asked members to input their ethnicity. In fact, it seems such recordkeeping would be important (albeit blurry at times) if the church is going to set goals for ethnic diversity and plans to assess its achievement of those goals.

No Racial or Ethnic Group Makes Up More Than 80 Percent of Those on the Worship Team

The ethnic diversity of the congregation is a significant metric, but scholars have discovered that the ethnic diversity of the worship team also matters to people. As Jamaal Williams and Timothy Jones point out, diversity onstage can repel those who prefer a monoethnic setting and can welcome those who prefer a multiethnic setting.[8] Seeing people like you onstage shows you have a place in the congregation of worshipers. "How can a church proclaim it believes heaven is open to all who believe and not have that 'all' represented on the platform?"[9]

Craig Garriott, pastor of Faith Christian Fellowship in Baltimore, explains that ethnic diversity onstage is important "just because of the public nature of that hour."[10] The public collaboration of multiple ethnicities demonstrates reconciliation and inclusion.

In *Many Colors: Cultural Intelligence for a Changing Church*, Soong-Chan Rah describes his experiences leading a multiethnic church. The majority group was Asian American, and as the senior pastor, he was the main person who spoke from the pulpit. Additionally, most of the worship leaders happened to also be Asian Americans. But he said that it was important to "increase participation from other ethnicities in all

7. Emerson, *People of the Dream*, 161.
8. Williams and Jones, *In Church as It Is in Heaven*.
9. Lewis-Giggetts, *The Integrated Church*, 146.
10. Ortiz, *One New People*, 52.

parts of the service" lest a newcomer assume that "all of the leaders of the church were Asian-American."[11] "After one of our White pastor staff began to give the announcements during the service, a White student at the church approached me to thank us for being sensitive to the wide variety of cultures and races that were in the church. Something as simple as ensuring every ethnicity had a visible presence proved to be an affirming action for one member of the church."[12]

Churches with a language-group posture have a unique opportunity to leverage this diversity on the worship team. They can share one another's talent! For example, musicians and singers in The Grove Español sometimes lead worship in the English services, and vice versa. One member of the Spanish worship team explained, "So we've had a lot of people from our Anglo church—our Anglo worship team—come and help support us in roles like leading worship, playing an instrument, even in the back, with the cameras and production. So they now have gotten to experience a Spanish service!"

Leti, who plays drums at a multiethnic church, explained that her worship team's diversity has shifted as "the dynamics of our church have shifted. Our pastor changed as well. . . . In the past, the church, the worship team was run by White people. And now we have—look at Wilson, is he mixed? What is he? Guatemalan? And Kati is Hispanic, and we have a diverse team now."

The diversity of staff *could* lead to diversity of musical styles. One world-renowned pianist, Alan, who splits his Sunday worship services between English and Spanish fellowships at his church, explained that in the English service, "On the platform, we have different cultures represented. We have certain Americans, we have deaf individuals, we have Latinos—I am not the only one—and the traditional White American member of the church, all together. One genre. The music? Very American. But those are baby steps going toward multiculturality." I (Ken) asked, "Do you think there would be another step after that with the music?" He responded,

> I've been intentional sometimes in the worship rehearsals to see the reactions. For example, we are in the middle of the rehearsal, we're

11. Rah, *Many Colors*, 171.
12. Rah, *Many Colors*, 171.

> singing [he begins to play the piano and sing a worship song] and I start doing [he changes the music style to a Latin rhythm] that salsa with the same worship. And I changed it just for fun. And the drummer—whose mom is Latina, and his dad is from Spain, and he's married to a Colombian—he immediately responded. But the others, they watch you, and we laugh and we celebrate. And I see that they are not ready yet. But they want something of that. . . . I'm starting to feel that they are starting to gradually become open to exploring different genres of worship that are beyond the bubble of the contemporary worship tradition.

I pushed Alan to articulate why he would want more Latin rhythms in the worship service, and he explained that "it's more theological." When congregations accept the diversity of worship styles, they live out Peter's vision in Acts 9 and 10, where he discovered that all cultures are "clean."

In our study, we never encountered church leaders who came close to describing a quota system for the diversity onstage. There was an *awareness* of the importance, and even intentionality in recruiting, but typically not an official position. Jeff, who is a pastor at Centerpoint—a multiethnic church in Colton, California—said, "We always try to make sure that our stage is representative of our people." Ray Washington, lead pastor of East Lake Community Church in Irmo, South Carolina, said that the worship leader "is mindful about making sure that it's not an all-White group of individuals singing and playing." Andi, who sings at The Grove, described it this way:

> There's never been a specific statement of, "We're seeking to be multidiverse or multiethnic." But I will say that the worship pastor has always said, "I love being able to see our worship team and how diverse we are." And it's not just ethnicity, but it's also differences in age. We have really young, eighteen-year-olds, all the way up to fifty or sixty. It was never something that was intentional. It just ended up happening to be that way. . . . And I think part of the reason why it's happening organically is because people can look up and see different people represented, and they're like, "Oh, it's not just geared toward the Anglo-Saxon. It is every different ethnicity, generation." And that invites people to be a part of that.

No Racial or Ethnic Group Makes Up More Than 80 Percent of the Leadership (Pastors, Staff, and Elders) in the Church

Having ethnic diversity also includes having a diverse leadership team. As Mark DeYmaz and Harry Li state, "To build a healthy multi-ethnic church, you must also empower diverse leaders, from the pulpit to the nursery and at every stop in between, vocational and volunteer leaders alike."[13] Yet should churches intentionally aim for such diversity? Does that mean setting quotas? DeYmaz and Li aren't sure it should go that far and suggest that "when it comes to staffing for diversity, intentionality is the middle ground between quota and wishful thinking."[14]

A key way for congregation members to feel welcomed is to have representation on the leadership team. As Mark Hearn notes, "We quickly discerned that to help visitors feel at home in the pew, we needed to put someone from their own language and culture on the platform."[15]

Daniel Hyun, pastor of the Village Church in Baltimore, discovered that he was a "stranger" to many in his community. He brought on staff individuals from various socioeconomic and cultural backgrounds, not just to have "token" leaders, but so that his own leadership style would be stretched and challenged at times.[16]

Derwin Gray cautions that having an ethnically diverse congregation without an intentionally ethnically diverse leadership team is a sign of dysfunction. "On the surface the increase in multiethnic congregations looks good. And some of it is good. However, as we get underneath the numbers, multiethnic megachurches are more likely the result of the perceived upward mobility of the megachurch. . . . It is not the result of a theological conviction and the inclusion of minority leadership."[17]

Yet ethnic diversity should start from the top. "The church that is called to work with African American men doesn't have to be led by

13. DeYmaz and Li, *Leading a Healthy Multi-Ethnic Church*, 46.
14. DeYmaz and Li, *Leading a Healthy Multi-Ethnic Church*, 46.
15. Hearn, *Technicolor*, 156–57.
16. Hyun, "Challenge and Blessing."
17. Gray, *Building a Multiethnic Church*, 19.

an African American man or even a predominantly African American congregation, but *must* have African American men in leadership positions."[18] Ethnic diversity in the leadership directly impacts who is willing to be part of the church. Yancey explains, "In the Lilly data the highest percentage of blacks that attended a church with no black clergy was 33 percent. The highest percentage of whites and Hispanics who were willing to attend churches without members of their own group in leadership was 50 percent."[19]

What are the journeys of leaders into racially diverse churches? Korie Little Edwards and Rebecca Kim's study of 120 leaders of racially diverse churches revealed that often they "grew up in churches where most if not all of the people in their congregations shared their ethnoracial identity."[20] But as they went to university or seminary, they encountered different leadership and worship styles and discovered that they no longer "fit" in their homogenous churches back home; some even felt alienated from their ethnic communities that they came from.[21] Additionally, many of these leaders either experienced or witnessed racial injustice.[22]

The diversity of elected volunteer leaders is also a factor. David Wise, pastor of Greenford Baptist Church in West London, England, noticed that most of the leaders in his church were older women. He instituted a leadership training group (LTG) to develop young leaders. Because his church was increasingly reaching immigrant communities from the Caribbean and Hong Kong, his LTG was highly diverse. This led to further diversity in the church leadership as well as in the membership.[23] The church went from 91 percent White British in 1987 to 33 percent White British in 2014.[24]

Pastor Mark DeYmaz shared with us that Mosaic Church of Central Arkansas is very intentional about having a diverse pastoral leadership team because of the added value:

18. Lewis-Giggetts, *The Integrated Church*, 65.
19. Yancey, *One Body, One Spirit*, 157.
20. Edwards and Kim, *Estranged Pioneers*, 38.
21. Edwards and Kim, *Estranged Pioneers*, 43.
22. Edwards and Kim, *Estranged Pioneers*, 17.
23. Wise, "Multi-Ethnic Local Church," 22.
24. Wise, "Multi-Ethnic Local Church," 208.

> We have a visionary leader, that's me; we have a pastoral shepherd leader, that's Harry; and we have an operations leader who forms and functions, that's Lawrence. Lawrence is Black, Harry's Chinese, and I'm White. So with all that in mind, the three of us act as one. When it comes to issues on the table that are more visionary of nature, we all discuss, talk, argue, fight, put our ideas on the table, but they look to me to summarize all that if the issue is vision. But if the issue is people and problems or shepherding, we look to Harry to do that. If it's operational, we look to Lawrence to do that. So we yield to one another in the strength of our gifting. We play as one.

Pastor Mark further explained that instead of viewing the other members on the pastoral leadership team as threats or competitors, this leadership style allows congregation members to seek counsel from a leader who can best relate to their specific situation. These are some of the benefits of having a pastoral leadership team that represents more than one specific culture:

> They see us as a team, and just like marriage, if there are any issues like, if someone doesn't like me, or they get sideways with me, they go to Harry. They see different people they like. It's not like, "I like Apollos or I like Paul," but it's kind of like that, because some people naturally gravitate to Lawrence whether it's because they're African American, whether it's because they have a military background, whether it's because they're born and raised in Arkansas, unlike me and Harry. It doesn't mean they don't like me or follow me or Harry, or that they don't respect us, it's just they would naturally form a relationship more with Lawrence—same thing with Harry, for a variety of reasons.

Images of the Church on the Website, Social Media, and Promotional Materials Have More Than One Ethnicity Represented

When perusing websites of multiethnic churches, it is not uncommon to find an array of faces that reflect the diverse makeup of the church. This includes images on the website, social media, PowerPoints, pictures, signs, and other visual media. "To promote a spirit of inclusion, planters and reformers must also pay attention to those little things that add up to create the look and feel of the whole."[25] Pastor Jeff, at Centerpoint Church in Colton, California, said the leadership asks, "Does the website authentically show you what you're going to see when you show up here? So our website, if you look at it, there's a diversity of people." The church leadership became aware that the video series they purchased was not representative of their area. Pastor Jeff related to us, "We noticed everyone's White in it. The houses are beautiful two-story homes with huge lawns. And we're like, 'That doesn't look like Colton. Yeah, just doesn't look like Colton.'"

Churches like Mosaic Church in Central Arkansas even ensure that their nursery and early childhood classrooms have "dolls of all colors": "Such considerations, though seemingly inconsequential, demonstrate to others a great deal about who we are and what we value."[26] In addition to images, various languages may be included in promotional materials, websites, and other written communication. Wheaton Bible Church in West Chicago, Illinois, ensures that all its signs and banners are displayed in both English and Spanish. Images in the sanctuary also promote ethnic diversity. First Baptist Church of Duluth, Georgia, has fifty-six permanently installed flags to represent the birth nations of those in the congregation.[27] Greenford Baptist Church (GBC) has flags from forty-seven nations on display as well as Chinese art depicting various Bible stories[28] and "various pieces of art reflecting different African styles and a large prominently displayed installation that feature[s] the name of God in 28 languages. Members of the GBC congregation contributed all of the art."[29]

Congregants told Wise that seeing their culture represented in flags and art reinforced to them that they truly belong in this church.[30] An interesting converse to this is the use of an American flag. A highly multicultural church in the Pacific Northwest, which has many foreign

25. DeYmaz, *Building a Healthy Multi-Ethnic Church*, 113.

26. DeYmaz, *Building a Healthy Multi-Ethnic Church*, 113.

27. Hearn, *Technicolor*, 49. Note when Hearn's book was published in 2017, the number was forty-seven flags.

28. Wise, "Multi-Ethnic Local Church," 147.

29. Wise, "Multi-Ethnic Local Church," 43.

30. Wise, "Multi-Ethnic Local Church," 149.

workers in its congregation, removed the American flag from the sanctuary several years ago. One member explained, "We wanted to show that our citizenship is in heaven." But we suspect there is more to it than that. In fact, his wife added, "One woman told me she would not have started coming to our church if there had been an American flag in there." This is a complex and controversial issue, but churches that are improving their cross-cultural posture should consider further research in their context. They may ask, "How do congregants who are in the United States on work visas interpret the display of the American flag in the sanctuary?"

To add to the controversy, some churches have discovered that ethnic diversity in the imagery around the church also requires diversity in depictions of Jesus, the disciples, and the early church. Charles Foster recounts a decision to diversify the imagery at Oakhurst Presbyterian Church in Decatur, Georgia: "After a prolonged and often heated discussion, the session of the congregation voted to darken the image of Jesus and some of the disciples in the stained-glass window over the choir loft in front and to leave the 'White' image of Jesus in the window over the back balcony."[31]

Although the level of ethnic diversity described in this chapter requires planning, churches need to be careful to avoid what Jessica Barron and Rhys Williams call "managed diversity."[32] This is when "church officials strategically manage the visibility of black volunteers, appropriate elements of urban blackness, and yet studiously avoid racialized cultural texts and religious practices within their congregation. The management of diversity legitimates the congregation as not being 'too White' but rather a diverse, authentic urban establishment that is appropriate for young, hip urban dwellers to enjoy."[33]

Surprisingly, managed diversity can also involve keeping images of people of color *off* the internet. Edwards and Kim describe two other instances of multiethnic churches where the pastors (one Asian American, one African American) keep their faces off any messaging,

31. Foster, *Embracing Diversity*, 32.
32. Barron and Williams, *The Urban Church Imagined*, 21.
33. Barron and Williams, *The Urban Church Imagined*, 73.

so that people will not assume that their churches are exclusively for ethnic minorities.[34]

People Experience Multiethnic Relationships in the Church

A benefit of multiethnic churches is that members can experience relationships with people who have different perspectives, experiences, and values. As Curtiss Paul DeYoung and his coauthors describe it, multiethnic congregations can "serve as gathering spaces where Whites and persons of color begin to see and relate to each other as human beings."[35] Similarly, Laurene Bowers explains that one "objective for the multicultural church is to teach parishioners . . . new patterns of relating to persons of other cultural groupings."[36] "Within the church setting, during worship, fellowship, and mission projects, individuals develop relationships and challenge and change their perception of themselves and others. They confront their fears concerning their interactions with people who are different from themselves; by reality-testing these fears and discovering that they have no basis in reality, they let go of them."[37]

Through various programs, Sunday school classes, events, fellowship, and even during worship, people who attend multiethnic churches have the opportunity to embrace the cultural Other. "The will to give ourselves to others and 'welcome' them, to readjust our identities to make space for them, is prior to any judgment about others, except that of identifying them in their humanity."[38]

Such an environment also requires goodwill and trust. Mark DeYmaz, pastor of Mosaic in Central Arkansas, said that although "cross-cultural relationships form the very foundation and fabric of a multi-ethnic church," such relationships may be difficult "because trust is not a commodity so easily assumed in an environment where people must interact with others different from themselves."[39]

34. Edwards and Kim, *Estranged Pioneers*, 75.
35. DeYoung et al., *United by Faith*, 134.
36. Bowers, *Becoming a Multicultural Church*, 121.
37. Bowers, *Becoming a Multicultural Church*, 121.
38. Volf, *Exclusion and Embrace*, 29.
39. DeYmaz, *Building a Healthy Multi-Ethnic Church*, 84.

CHAPTER SUMMARY

Churches are increasingly experiencing ethnic diversity in their leadership teams, in the worship bands, and in the pews. While some churches are intentional about being multiethnic, others have become diverse as a natural result of demographic changes in their towns. Ethnic diversity does not automatically result in strong interethnic relationships, but churches can prioritize such cohesion—especially in fellowship groups and service groups. Additionally, the presence of multiple ethnicities does not necessarily result in the expression of multiple cultures. Multiculturality was discussed as a separate domain in chapter 1. To avoid the tendency to be multiethnic but monocultural, churches should be careful to avoid "tokenism" and ensure that the voices of all ethnic groups in the church are heard.

Things to Watch for with Ethnic Diversity

- Create spaces where everyone truly feels welcomed and has a sense of belonging rather than being treated as a token.
- Be mindful of privilege and power dynamics that may exist more prominently in the different ethnic groups.
- Ensure that various cultural groups feel accurately and adequately represented in the leadership team, during worship services, and in promotional materials.
- Recognize that building trust and relationships among various ethnic groups may take time.

REFLECTION QUESTIONS

1. Think about the ethnic makeup at your church. How did it become like that?
2. What steps does your church take to increase multiethnic interactions?
3. What steps does your church take to increase multiethnic representation?

For Further Reading on Ethnic Diversity

Gray, Derwin. *Building a Multiethnic Church: A Gospel Vision of Love, Grace, and Reconciliation in a Divided World*. Nelson, 2021.

Gray, Derwin. *The High-Definition Leader: Building Multiethnic Churches in a Multiethnic World*. Nelson, 2015.

Edwards, Korie Little. *The Elusive Dream: The Power of Race in Interracial Churches*. Oxford University Press, 2008.

Edwards, Korie Little. "The Multiethnic Church Movement Hasn't Lived Up to Its Promise." *Christianity Today*, March 2021. https://www.christianitytoday.com/2021/02/race-diversity-multiethnic-church-movement-promise/.

Edwards, Korie Little, and Rebecca Y. Kim. *Estranged Pioneers: Race, Faith, and Leadership in a Diverse World*. Oxford University Press, 2024.

Emerson, Michael O. *People of the Dream: Multiracial Congregations in the United States*. Princeton University Press, 2006.

Gushiken, Kevin M. "Cultivating Healthy Discipleship Settings in Multi-Ethnic Churches." *Transformation: An International Journal of Holistic Mission Studies* 32, no. 1 (2015): 17–26.

Gushiken, Kevin M. "Is a Christian Identity Compatible with an Ethnic Identity? An Exploration of Ethnic Identity Negotiation Influences and Implications for Multi-Ethnic Congregations." *Christian Education Journal* 11, no. 1 (2014): 33–44.

Ince, Irwyn L., Jr. *The Beautiful Community: Unity, Diversity, and the Church at Its Best*. InterVarsity, 2015.

Rah, Soong-Chan. *Many Colors: Cultural Intelligence for a Changing Church*. Moody, 2010.

Measuring Your Church's Cross-Cultural Posture

The Cross-Cultural Posture Index and Model

These five MOTIVEs (Multiculturality, Oneness, Togetherness, Inclusionary Vision, Ethnic Diversity) allow us to develop a composite measure called the Cross-Cultural Posture Assessment Tool (CPAT) described below. Your church's score on the CPAT results in one of seven cross-cultural postures (note that some churches end up with a "hybrid" score):

1. Shared-Space Posture
2. Monocultural/Monoethnic Posture
3. Advocate Posture
4. Multiethnic Posture
5. Language-Group Posture
6. Reconciling Posture
7. Culture-Blending Posture

Your score in each of these five indices on the CPAT can prompt you to reflect on your posture and may help you identify any areas you want to improve in developing your cross-cultural ministry.

But before we present the tool for measuring your church's cross-cultural posture, we want to explain some of our terms in this assessment tool.

Why We Use the Term "Postures"

Churches are defined by much more than their cross-cultural posture, so it is inaccurate to refer to a church as a "monocultural church" or a "multiethnic church." In fact, we have not found a single example of a church that officially describes itself as a "monocultural church." And we are giving the benefit of the doubt here. Many churches with a monocultural posture are unintentionally so, though they may make decisions in staffing, programming, and teaching that perpetuate a monocultural/monoethnic constituency. But the members and leaders in these churches have so much more to say about their churches than that they are monocultural. They describe their church's heart for serving the community, for making disciples, and for glorifying God. So when we remember to be careful about our wording, we describe such churches as "churches with a monocultural posture," not "monocultural churches." This is the same with the other postures.

Although this study focused on the cross-cultural postures of fifteen churches, other lenses could be applied to those same churches to examine many other aspects, including leadership development, discipleship models, sending of missionaries, or many other aspects of ecclesiology. In fact, the churches we visited to research this book describe themselves in the following ways *besides* their inclusionary vision:

- "We exist to glorify God by making disciples who make disciples who love God, love one another, love our neighbors, and love the nations."[1] (Wheaton Bible Church, Wheaton, Illinois)
- "Centerpoint Church is a life-giving church in Colton, California, with great worship music, practical messages, and a kids' program that your kids will LOVE!"[2]

1. Wheaton Bible Church, accessed February 7, 2026, https://www.wheatonbible.org/.
2. Centerpoint Church, accessed February 7, 2026, https://www.centerpointchurch.church/.

- "Mosaic [Grand Rapids, Michigan] was birthed out of the biblical passion to see the church become the 'one new humanity' Scripture tells us was Jesus's purpose."[3]
- "We are a church being changed by God to reach all people."[4] (The Grove Community Church, Riverside, California)

Additionally, while we have found churches that describe themselves as multicultural or multiethnic, churches that have a multiethnic posture (according to the CPAT) are, by the tool's own definition, low on inclusionary vision. Becoming ethnically diverse is not necessarily a core value within that posture; it may happen organically, or even "accidentally." Issues of inclusion may not be addressed in the teaching, planning, and programming. So it would be a misrepresentation to call such churches "multiethnic churches," as if this accurately captures the church's character. Again, members and leaders within this posture have rich descriptions of their church's heart for discipleship, service, and evangelism, and ethnic diversity is one of many other ingredients in the church's makeup. So when we are most accurate, we would not *define* such churches as "multiethnic churches." Instead, we would say they have a multiethnic posture.

This careful wording can be applied to each of the postures, although a culture-blending church—ahem, *a church with a culture-blending posture*—is likely to be far more conscious of its cross-cultural posture than a church with a shared-space posture.

The MOTIVEs Are on a Continuum, Not Binary

In addition to remembering that a church's cross-cultural posture is only one ingredient in its makeup, it's important to notice that the MOTIVEs are not binary. Churches are not easily put into boxes such as "inclusionary or noninclusionary," "multicultural or monocultural," "ethnically diverse or homogenous." Instead, churches have higher or lower degrees of inclusionary vision, higher or lower

3. Mosaic Church Grand Rapids, "Our Story," accessed February 7, 2026, https://mosaicgr.org.

4. The Grove Community Church, "Welcome," accessed February 7, 2026, https://www.thegrove.cc/.

degrees of multiculturality, and so on. That's why the assessment tool uses a Likert scale from 0 to 3, and each index results in a composite of the five items, resulting in a score *somewhere between* 0 and 15. In our dataset, only eleven participants rated their churches as zero on the multiculturality index, only three as zero on the oneness index, only six as a zero on the togetherness index, only three as a zero on the inclusionary vision index, and only five as a zero on the ethnic diversity index. Participants see *some* levels of each of these MOTIVEs at their churches. Again, this is why it is important to emphasize that it's not accurate to say that a church either has or does not have oneness, togetherness, and so on. Instead, this assessment tool looks for "high togetherness," "high oneness," and so on. By a "high" score we mean a composite score of 12 or higher out of 15.[5]

Churches' MOTIVEs Change over Time

The five MOTIVEs in churches are not static; they change, sometimes unintentionally. Centerpoint Church in Colton, California, tried out simultaneous Spanish translation (higher multiculturality) and then abandoned that strategy (moving toward lower multiculturality) because its constituency was largely composed of English-speaking second- and third-generation immigrants. East Lake Community Church—a predominantly White congregation in Irmo, South Carolina—had a Black gospel choir (higher multiculturality) until the choir director passed away. Now the worship is lower on multiculturality.

But if the MOTIVEs change, they can be intentionally increased too. East Lake has lower multiculturality for now, until their worship talent includes those who can incorporate other worship styles. One member told us, "As far as the worship, it's pretty much predominantly one way of worshiping. I like to say it's the Elevation[6] kind of approach. We do sing some hymns, but it's more of the upbeat

5. We also tried lowering the threshold to 11 out of 15, but the change had little impact on the resulting distribution of postures in the dataset.

6. The reference is to Elevation Worship. See https://www.elevationworship.com/.

hymns. We don't really go into any other realm, any other cultural worship. So I don't think that's something that we've done before. And I think that's something they want to get to."

Leaders at The Grove and at Centerpoint also expressed a desire to make the worship more representative of Latin rhythms or Black gospel. What makes the CPAT so useful is that you can change your MOTIVEs!

Cross-Cultural Posture Assessment Tool

The CPAT allows you to measure five factors that contribute to your church's cross-cultural ministry. The score on these five indices will result in one of seven postures (see the scoring key at the end of this assessment).

Instructions

Think about your church, answer the twenty-five questions, and then use the scoring table below to determine your church's cross-cultural posture.

Multiculturality Index

After each statement, put a number to indicate how much you agree or disagree with the statement.

Strongly disagree: 0; Somewhat disagree: 1; Somewhat agree: 2; Strongly agree: 3

Answer the following by considering all congregations and campuses represented by your church:

1. Worship songs are in more than one language each week. _____
2. The pastoral leadership styles represent more than one cultural background. _____
3. Sermons are regularly delivered in more than one language. _____

4. The worship services represent more than one cultural background each week. _____
5. The programs and events at the church represent more than one cultural background. _____

If your church's score is 12 or higher in this factor, give your church an M in the scoring table below.

Oneness Index

After each statement, put a number to indicate how much you agree or disagree with the statement:

Strongly disagree: 0; Somewhat disagree: 1; Somewhat agree: 2; Strongly agree: 3

1. There is one leadership team (pastors, staff, elders) for all congregations/campuses in this church. _____
2. There is one budget for all congregations/campuses in this church. _____
3. There is one vision for all congregations/campuses in this church. _____
4. There is one growth plan, including sermon series and membership process, for all congregations/campuses in this church. _____
5. There is one major communication channel going to all ethnic/language groups in all congregations/campuses in this church. _____

If your church's score is 12 or higher in this factor, give your church an O in the scoring table below.

Togetherness Index

After each statement, put a number to indicate how much you agree or disagree with the statement:

Strongly disagree: 0; Somewhat disagree: 1; Somewhat agree: 2; Strongly agree: 3

1. The weekly worship services include all of the language, cultural, and ethnic groups in the church worshiping together. _____
2. The children and youth programs include all language, cultural, and ethnic groups in the church together. _____
3. Discipleship groups are composed of all the language, cultural, and ethnic groups in the church together. _____
4. The fellowship events throughout the year are for all of the language, cultural, and ethnic groups in the church together. _____
5. The service and outreach programs are composed of all the language, cultural, and ethnic groups in the church together. _____

If your church's score is 12 or higher in this factor, give your church a T in the scoring table below.

Inclusionary Vision Index

After each statement, put a number to indicate how much you agree or disagree with the statement:

Strongly disagree: 0; Somewhat disagree: 1; Somewhat agree: 2; Strongly agree: 3

1. Inclusion of various races/ethnicities is expressly part of this church's vision or mission statement. _____
2. Pastoral staff regularly addresses issues related to ethnic or racial inclusion. _____
3. The church has programming to address ethnic or racial inclusion. _____
4. The church has aimed its programming to respond to demographic changes in the neighborhood. _____
5. People in the church care about ethnic or racial inclusion. _____

If your church's score is 12 or higher in this factor, give your church an IV in the scoring table below.

Ethnic Diversity Index

After each statement, put a number to indicate how much you agree or disagree with the statement:

Strongly disagree: 0; Somewhat disagree: 1; Somewhat agree: 2; Strongly agree: 3

1. No ethnic group makes up more than 80 percent of those gathered for worship. _____
2. No ethnic group makes up more than 80 percent of those leading worship. _____
3. No ethnic group makes up more than 80 percent of the leadership team (pastors, staff, and elders). _____
4. People experience multiethnic relationships here. _____
5. The images of the church on the website, social media, and promotional materials have more than one ethnicity represented. _____

If your church's score is 12 or higher in this factor, give your church an E in the scoring table below.

Cross-Cultural Posture Scoring Table

If your church scored 12 or higher in Multiculturality, put an M below	If your church scored 12 or higher in Oneness, put an O below	If your church scored 12 or higher in Togetherness, put a T below	If your church scored 12 or higher in Inclusionary Vision, put an IV below	If your church scored 12 or higher in Ethnic Diversity, put an E below

Cross-Cultural Posture Scoring Key

1. High M: Shared-Space Posture
2. High O (T optional): Monocultural/Monoethnic Posture
3. High High O+IV (T optional): Advocate Posture
4. High O+T+E: Multiethnic Posture
5. High M+O (IV, E optional): Language-Group Posture
6. High O+T+IV+E: Reconciling Posture
7. High M+O+T+IV+E: Culture-Blending Posture
8. Hybrid: If the score includes a combination that is not listed in numbers 1–7 above, the church is a hybrid, meaning it incorporates aspects of these various postures but does not fit neatly into a box.

Preliminary Results of the Cross-Cultural Posture Assessment Tool

We deployed the survey to 214 church members of 131 churches in order to test for the reliability, validity, and "goodness of fit" of the CPAT developed above. Part 1 built a case for the content validity of this instrument, and the book's conclusion discusses the "goodness of fit." Below, we briefly cover the internal reliability of the CPAT, and we discuss how some findings from the preliminary survey relate to criterion validity.

The Cronbach's alpha score is used to indicate internal reliability of a survey instrument. The Cronbach's alphas for the five indices are listed here:

1. Multicultural index: .83
2. Oneness index: .90
3. Togetherness index: .87
4. Inclusionary Vision index: .87
5. Ethnic Diversity index: .92

A score above .70 is considered internally reliable, so this suggests that the five indices have high reliability.

Criterion Validity: People Overestimate and Underestimate the MOTIVEs

On several occasions, we deployed the Cross-Cultural Posture Assessment Tool to several members of the same church in order to test for a type of criterion validity called "concurrent validity" (specifically, does the survey instrument yield the same result as what we already knew, by participant observation, to be the church's cross-cultural posture?). While many respondents correctly identified their church's posture with the CPAT, we discovered that some people—likely those who are sensitized to issues of cultural inclusion—underestimate their church's level of inclusionary vision, multiculturality, and ethnic diversity. For example, we may have known in advance (by head count) that a church's constituency meets the "80 percent rule," but some respondents gave a low score on ethnic diversity for that church. Or we knew that the church has services in multiple languages, but this escaped the consciousness of some participants. On the other hand, some respondents who felt very positive regard toward their church overestimated their church's MOTIVEs, indicating, for example, high levels of multilingualism when we already knew (by participant observation) that the church is almost exclusively monolingual.

This divergence in perspectives actually presents church leaders with an opportunity: Discuss the MOTIVEs. Have key members take the Cross-Cultural Posture Assessment Tool, and then discuss the results as a group. See where other stakeholders have high or low opinions of the church's MOTIVEs. This will help you determine which areas need to be improved.

PART 2

Seven Cross-Cultural Postures

Although monocultural and monoethnic churches are still the norm, there has been a significant increase in the number of multicultural or multiethnic churches throughout North America. As a matter of fact, through our research, we have come to find that there are many different variations of multicultural/multiethnic churches. In the next section, we further explain seven different cross-cultural postures. Although there is a strong biblical case for all five MOTIVEs discussed in part 1 (Multiculturality, Oneness, Togetherness, Inclusionary Vision, Ethnic Diversity), we recognize that no single posture is better than another. As Charles Foster puts it,

> I do not take the position that the multicultural congregation should become the model for congregational life in the future. Indeed, our study of culturally and racially diverse congregations only underscored the impossibility of such an assumption. The notion of a single model for multicultural congregations, in fact, contradicts the very notion of diversity that they embrace. Regional (geographic) differences in the history of racial and cultural relationship further limit any possibility to find or develop a single model for the multicultural congregation.[1]

1. Foster, *Embracing Diversity*, xii.

In part 2, we describe each of the cross-cultural postures, and we include observations from our visits to churches that fit each of these postures. We also evaluate situations where each posture is a good fit and where it can be problematic. Then we discuss each posture in light of biblical descriptions of cross-cultural postures in the early church. Lastly, we provide reflection questions and summaries in each chapter. Keep in mind that the best posture for a church depends on its specific call, context, and constituency. The New Testament describes each of these postures at some point in the development of the early church. Therefore, each of these postures has a biblical basis.[2]

2. Manuel Ortiz connects the following postures to Scripture: (1) a church that pursues multiculturality for the sake of the Great Commission is connected to Matthew 28; (2) a church that is committed to racial reconciliation (here, the advocate posture) is connected to Ephesians 2–4; (3) a church that is committed to having various ethnicities worship together is connected to Acts 2; (4) churches that are experiencing demographic shifts are connected to Acts 11 and 13. See Ortiz, *One New People*.

CHAPTER 6

The Shared-Space Posture

Characteristics of a Shared-Space Posture

Acts 2:1–41

Strengths:
Support for fledgling congregations

Weaknesses:
Low cohesion; paternalism

Context:
Declining memberships at an established church; multicultural neighborhood

Calling:
Ensure stability of the church and facilities; support fledgling congregations

Constituency:
Monocultural established church

Kenneth Nehrbass

Chapter Goals

By the end of this chapter, you should be able to do the following:

- identify advantages and disadvantages of sponsoring a congregation from a different cultural/ethnic group
- reflect on ways your church can better partner with congregations from other ethnic/cultural groups in your area

As many predominantly White mainline churches wane in membership numbers, their once-bustling campuses and sanctuaries are now severely overbuilt.[1] The membership in many of these churches has gotten so thin, in fact, that the churches are looking for additional avenues of revenue to maintain their costly campuses. Meanwhile, fledgling ethnic congregations—usually with slim budgets—are on the lookout for space to worship and even to grow. This is where the shared-space posture may be relevant. The shared-space posture is a partnership between congregations to use the same facilities. There are two or more church services each Sunday in different languages and styles. Typically, each congregation maintains separate budgets, children's programs, meetings, and leadership structures.

In fact, the shared-space posture is common. One study of 214 churches in the Boston metropolitan area showed that 32 percent of churches shared their space with another congregation; and of these, 95 percent of the host congregations were from a different ethnic background than their guests.[2] A US Congregational Life Survey in 2008/9 revealed that over 25 percent of churches pointed to revenues from space-sharing as a significant part of their income.[3]

Of course, it's not just about income. (And if it were just about income, we would not consider this a cross-cultural posture.) A

1. Mainline refers to American Baptist Churches USA (ABCUSA), the Evangelical Lutheran Church of America, the Presbyterian Church (USA), the United Methodist Church, and the Episcopal Church. Between 1960 and 2010, the number of people attending mainline churches in the United States dropped from 27 million to 20 million (see Barna Group, "The State of Mainline Churches").

2. Emmanuel Gospel Center, "Shared Worship Space."

3. Methodist Theological School in Ohio, "Benefits of Space-Sharing."

mixed-methods study of congregations ($n = 100$) revealed five major motivations for the shared-space posture:

1. Community need
2. Congregational need
3. Finances
4. God's mission
5. Underutilized asset[4]

If sharing space were just about income, financially well-off congregations would have little incentive to take on the liabilities and difficulties of allowing other congregations to use their campuses. However, some churches, like the First Christian Reformed Church in Hanford, California, share their space free of charge. Lambert Sikkema, co-pastor of the church, explained, "It's all about Kingdom Asset Management. . . . Is the Kingdom of God getting maximum benefit from a God-given asset? If not, what more could be done to utilize space and facilities to an ever-greater extent for the advancement of the Kingdom?"[5]

This shared-space relationship can be described as "temporary sponsorship,"[6] or when it is a bit more permanent, "alliance."[7] Mark DeYmaz and Harry Li refer to the renter-landlord arrangement as "Intended Exclusion: Us and Them."[8]

Although the shared-space posture has low togetherness, this does not mean there is *no* togetherness. In fact, the "managed" level of togetherness is seen as a blessing. A member at The Fount explained: "I think one of the wonderful things about having a shared campus is the fact that you can do things together. So it usually starts with the youth—actually, the youth of the various groups go camping, do fundraising, all of those types of things. . . . It's really exciting to see, meet, communicate, and worship with people that you know,

4. Pomroy, "Church Rental Property Q&A."
5. Hamstra, "Why We Don't Want to Rent Space."
6. Choi, "Multicultural Church," 67.
7. Choi, "Multicultural Church," 66.
8. DeYmaz and Li, *Ethnic Blends*, 101.

English may not be their primary language, but to learn about their culture just by witnessing even how they worship."

The Difficulties of the Shared-Space Posture

The danger of the shared-space posture is that rental space can be arranged without fundamentally addressing the DNA of the church. The congregation may have little buy-in. Jonathan Downie, a champion of multilingual churches, is concerned that the shared-space posture does not require enough of the sponsors. "Neither church is required to make any great changes or sacrifices. As long as the service times line up, chairs are left in the right place, and rooms are clean and tidy, there is unlikely to be any real tension. In addition, the church with the building can feel that they are doing something to reach people from a different background, with a minimum of initial effort."[9]

Due to the low level of cohesion in this posture, cultural differences can lead to grudges. Speaking about the multicultural situation in Great Britain, Harvey Kwiyani recounted, "An African congregation in the Midlands lost their rental license in 2018 because, as the official statement said, they were too loud, especially on Friday nights when they had their vigils. When they pushed to find out the real reason for having their license revoked, it became clear that the issue was the 'smelly' foods they cooked in the church's kitchen."[10]

The difficulty of "shared altars" is most prominent in this posture. Restoration Ministries of Greater Cleveland (formerly Covenant Baptist Church) in Euclid, Ohio, rents its space from a Catholic church. Senior pastor Christine Smith explained that her congregation is not allowed to use the "sacred space" and instead must gather in the education wing. Originally, they were not allowed to even post a sign advertising their church.[11] One pastor of a small congregation that rents its facilities from a declining mainline church told us that the host church is "all about preservation and making sure the facility

9. Downie, *Multilingual Church*, 38.
10. Kwiyani, *Multicultural Kingdom*, 127.
11. Smith, "Laying a Foundation," 102.

is utilized in a very systematic way. But for us, our church, we're more like, 'If the Holy Spirit leads, we do it.' I mean, we're using the facility for the mission. The facility isn't the mission, you know?"

It is clear that with sharing space, communication is key. The Fount in Fountain Valley, California, is host to three other congregations. Bill, a longtime lay leader at The Fount, explained that a liaison committee helps address some of these issues: "It's very important to have a liaison committee, because there are just the little things about sharing space—relating to storage, relating to the office, relating to keys, relating to all those things where there needs to be good communication. And overall, it's worked very well. We meet . . . once a month and talk about programs, talk about the calendar. That's very important so that the space is available for the various uses of the different congregations."

As we saw in previous chapters, such collaboration is common in churches with high oneness and high togetherness. But this level of co-planning may not be obvious to churches with a shared-space posture—until it becomes necessary to create such a liaison committee.

The shared-space posture can also breed fears of sheep-stealing. A pastor we interviewed has rented facilities at various churches and believes that the significant cultural difference between his congregation and his current host church helps reduce fears of competition. His congregation is highly multicultural but rents facilities at a declining, predominantly White church: "They don't have any fear of competition. When you start partnering with these older churches, if it's the same language, especially, and a similarity in culture and tradition, there can be this fear of competition. So if our church was elderly, White, I'm sure our host church would feel that in some sort of way. . . . And if they were to steal our sheep, and they went to the 9:00 a.m. service, I don't think our people would last that long there. And that congregation wouldn't know how to serve them either."

Acts 2:1–41: A Biblical Example of the Shared-Space Posture

The shared-space posture reflects the Holy Spirit coming down at Pentecost in Acts 2. Pentecost was a Jewish feast that celebrated the firstfruits of the wheat harvest that were presented to God. Furthermore, Pentecost also marked the day when the law was given to Israel. Great numbers of people traveled to Jerusalem to celebrate the feast. It was then, "when the day of Pentecost arrived," that all the disciples were gathered in one place: "And suddenly there came from heaven a sound like a mighty rushing wind, and it filled the entire house where they were sitting. And divided tongues as of fire appeared to them and rested on each one of them. And they were all filled with the Holy Spirit and began to speak in other tongues as the Spirit gave them utterance" (Acts 2:2–4).

Acts 2 goes on to say that Jews from every nation who had come to Jerusalem heard the sound and gathered around. What was even more remarkable, however, was that each person heard their own dialect spoken by "Galileans," who would not have been familiar with these various languages.

While pastors occasionally suggest that Pentecost was a reversal of the tower of Babel, that is not actually what happened in Acts 2. A monoculture was not created. The Christians from various backgrounds maintained their distinct languages.[12] What united them was the object of their worship and their shared experience of encountering the Holy Spirit.

This passage beautifully illustrates the gathering of various languages and peoples in one place. What's particularly interesting, however, is that while the Holy Spirit could have given those present the gift of interpretation to understand a single language, instead the Holy Spirit empowered the believers to speak in many languages, allowing each person to hear the gospel in their own tongue. Heterogeneity was maintained.

As seen in Acts 2, the shared-space posture enables people from various ethnic backgrounds to gather in the same worship space while worshiping freely according to their own linguistic and cultural expressions.

12. Marzouk, *Intercultural Church*, 135–38.

CHAPTER SUMMARY

A growing number of churches are sharing their facilities with congregations from different ethnolinguistic backgrounds. There is high multiculturality on campus, but low oneness and low togetherness. These shared-space arrangements span from simply a landlord-renter model to a sponsorship model. While this posture introduces congregations to cross-cultural ministry and can foster relationships across cultural boundaries, the shared altars (or even shared kitchens) cause challenges, requiring significant grace from all parties involved.

Things to Watch for with the Shared-Space Posture

- Watch out for grumbling (Phil. 2:14; James 5:9).
- Be honest about power dynamics that might be involved.
- Be aware of cultural differences, which may involve differences in communication styles, expressions, spatial etiquette, and time.

A Sunday at The Fount

I (Ken) drive through the quiet suburbs of Orange County, California, and see a sign for The Fount on a grass field, along with a few buildings with an architectural style that clearly signals "established denominational church" to me. I easily find a place to park and enter the sanctuary. A greeter hands me a bulletin for The Fount. I notice an altar with a large Bible on it and a cross behind the altar—both covered in purple liturgical cloths, because it is the liturgical season of Lent. There are candles on the altar, which, in the busier days of the church, were lighted by an acolyte wearing a white robe. The choir loft has been replaced by a drum set that is surrounded by Plexiglas. And as I hear the organist playing the prelude, I wonder when the drum set is used.

The organist leads the congregation in an opening hymn. Most read the lyrics from the television screens, but some have brought their hymnals from home. I notice that hymnals are no longer found underneath the seats in the sanctuary. About twenty of the one hundred seats are filled. All are Anglo, except the pianist and singer, who are both of Asian descent. We then sing "Waymaker" and "Blessed Assurance."

A worship leader reads from the Gospel of John and from the Old Testament.

In addition to sharing its facilities, The Fount—reminiscent of early United Methodist Church (UMC) traditions—shares its pastor with another struggling UMC congregation nearby. Thirty years ago, both congregations had multiple staff on the payroll, but now neither can pay a full-time salary. The pastor has a "two-point charge" and is preaching this Sunday at the other congregation. A certified lay leader preaches here today on the role of the Holy Spirit. The sermon covers many heady topics, including the economic, relational, and ontological Trinity. He relies on some Greek and follows many Old Testament references in the New Testament. He explains that the role of the Holy Spirit is to guide us into truth and ends the sermon with an impassioned plea to hear God's voice. He also suggests that we obtain a MacArthur Study Bible and use the Blue Letter Bible online.

The music director performs a highly skilled offertory on the piano while singing. The organist starts the Doxology, and the congregation sings from memory. The time dedicated to "passing the peace" is longer than usual and is long enough to shake hands with everyone in the room.

The time for prayer requests dedicates equal time to recognizing anyone's need in the room. Four ask for prayer for a relative's health. The lay leader prays a prayer of supplication, and the congregation ends with the Lord's Prayer.

By this point, I hear the Hispanic congregation practicing for the 10:30 service.

We are dismissed outside and eat donuts and drink coffee under the gazebo, which I notice is twenty-five feet from where a table is set up for snacks and coffee for the Hispanic congregation.

At exactly 10:30, the Spanish service, CIMA, begins in the former youth lounge. I notice banners hanging on the walls that declare the church's values in Spanish: Service, Fellowship, Growth. I note that both praise songs are contemporary Christian music songs that have been translated into English. The worship band is composed of three singers, a bass guitarist, an electric guitarist, and a drummer. I also notice bongos on the stage but did not see them played today.

Without any announcement, half of the forty people in attendance file out of the room, and I can tell by the ages that this must be for children's ministry. There is a time of Communion, and I discover that congregants have grabbed a cup-and-bread combo set before being seated.

The pastor's sermon is also highly exegetical and relies on commentaries and Greek words. The sermon is from Mark 6:45–52, and the pastor focuses on the theme of waiting on God, even during times of turbulence. As the service ends, I realize that the New Life congregation should be starting in the worship hall by now.

I step outside and see that some are able to grab donuts that were brought for the Anglo service earlier, and someone from New Life has set down a stack of egg rolls that are in high demand.

The New Life service starts a bit late, so I was able to juggle going to CIMA and New Life. I enter the sanctuary and discover that this is when the drum set behind the Plexiglas is used. An Afro-Caribbean drummer plays, as guitarists of Cambodian descent lead worship along with an Anglo singer. I do not recognize all of the songs, but they are of contemporary Christian music style.

Communion is led by Pastor Kim and her husband, who lead the Vietnamese constituency of New Life. She addresses the congregation in English, and he addresses us in Vietnamese. We all come forward for the bread and grape juice.

After Communion, Pastor Paul Park—a second-generation Korean—introduces himself and the church. He refers to it as a "multicultural, multiethnic, and multilingual congregation" because there is "Vietnamese, Khmer, and English spoken here, so that you have an idea of what heaven will be like."

Pastor Paul asks us to greet our neighbors by telling them what one of our "guilty pleasures" is. I admit that mine is chocolate cheesecake, and my neighbor says that hers is coffee. I note that the eighty in attendance are of all ages—mixed-race couples, Black families, Cambodian families, and Vietnamese families. I recognize that the older Vietnamese folks are dressed to the nines, as is typical of their generation. I am less familiar with Cambodian dress styles, but I believe that many in the older generation are dressed traditionally. The second-generation youth in the room are dressed more like the other high school students in the city.

True to Pastor Paul's promise that the church is multicultural, Pastor Khan, who preaches in Khmai in a separate classroom the other Sundays of the month, preaches the first Sunday of the month in English to the whole group. He preaches for about fifteen minutes on the book of James, mentioning that in times of conflict we should focus on the Word of God. He also mentions that the Cambodian New Year is coming on April 17. Pastor Paul then preaches from James 4:6–10 on the blood of Christ. He says that "pride builds walls we aren't meant to have." His sermon delivery style is impassioned hortatory.

Then two younger Cambodian ushers—one carrying a baby—pass the offering bucket, while a QR code appears on the screen for members to give online.

A choir sings an Indigenous Khmai hymn to a musical track that has drums, keyboard, and chimes.

Pastor Paul ends the service by mentioning that they have bundles of small booklets in Vietnamese and English called "Heaven or Hell" for congregants to pass out in their neighborhoods.

Why the Shared-Space Posture Makes Sense for The Fount

The Fount nears the border of Santa Ana (with a large Hispanic population) and Garden Grove (with a large Vietnamese population). In the last half of the twentieth century, the church had several hundred in attendance. Among the many programs offered, there was a bustling musical theater program, and the church ran a ministry to the homeless where guests could pray and study Scripture, shower, do laundry, work on bicycle repair, get haircuts, and eat breakfast.

Several decades ago, the church attracted professionals who worked in aerospace at nearby Boeing, McDonnell Douglas, or Raytheon. Others were health-care providers, teachers, or entrepreneurs. Real estate has become expensive in Orange County, and home prices in the neighborhood of The Fount are well over one million dollars.

As American Christians shifted their allegiance from denominational to nondenominational churches, the church started a contemporary worship service. But it could not keep up with the trends. Attendance dwindled from 300 to 200 to 100, and then to the point where the only children in attendance were those of one of the staff members.

Keep in mind that an expensive real estate market makes it difficult for fledgling churches to find space. The Fount has always offered its facilities to ministries in the neighborhood. In the 1980s, it shared its space with a Jewish temple, a preschool, and the Boy Scouts. It later shared space with additional ethnically diverse congregations. Now the predominantly Anglo "legacy" congregation meets at 9:00 a.m.; a Spanish congregation called CIMA (in reference to the Spanish word for a mountaintop) rents the former youth lounge at 10:00 a.m.; a multicultural, multiethnic congregation called New Life rents the sanctuary at 11:30 a.m.; and while New Life finishes up a shared meal each week on the patio, a Vietnamese congregation rents the sanctuary at 1:30 p.m. While there is much goodwill among the various congregations, they do not share budgets, branding, communication channels, or leadership teams. And while individual members (or the leaders) may value ethnic diversity, the congregations have not mutually agreed on a shared commitment of oneness, let alone togetherness. The shared-space posture makes sense for The Fount for the following reasons:

- Dwindling and aging congregation that owns the facility
- Fledgling ethnic church start-ups
- Expensive real estate market
- Different aspirations of the lead pastors of each congregation
- Vast cultural differences between the congregations; ideological, denominational differences

REFLECTION QUESTIONS

1. What are the advantages and disadvantages of sponsoring a fledgling church from a different ethnic/cultural group?
2. If your church shares space with a congregation from another culture and language group, how can you increase the interaction so that you can develop cross-cultural relationships?

3. If your church shares space with a congregation from another culture or language group, how can your congregation gain the benefit of hearing the spiritual insights and biblical interpretations from the other congregation?

CHAPTER 7

The Monocultural/ Monoethnic Posture

Characteristics of a Monocultural/ Monoethnic Posture

1 Peter 2:9

Context:
Could be in a monocultural or ethnically diverse neighborhood

Calling:
Reach the people they know best in their native language

Constituency:
Monocultural congregation

Kenneth Nehrbass

Chapter Goals

By the end of this chapter, you should be able to do the following:

- understand why a church might intentionally choose to remain monocultural or monoethnic
- identify some of the challenges and limitations of remaining a monocultural or monoethnic church

A church that does not score high on multiculturality, ethnic diversity, or inclusionary vision, but that scores high in oneness, is likely a monocultural/monoethnic church. The monocultural/monoethnic posture is the "normal" approach for nearly 75 percent of American churches. Despite this high level of monoculturality, a survey of 1,003 American Protestant churchgoers revealed that 69 percent believe that their church is doing enough to be ethnically diverse.[1] Many Christians are in monocultural churches and do not see a need for things to change.

As Curtiss Paul DeYoung and his coauthors point out, there are various reasons churches are monocultural—some more biblically sound than others.[2]

- Some churches are monoethnic because their entire city is largely monoethnic. "Scripture, therefore, does not frown upon monoethnic churches as if they are somehow less healthy than their cosmopolitan counterparts. Churches may be mono-ethnic if that is the natural byproduct of their righteous, contextualized ministries."[3]
- Globally, some churches are monoethnic because they actively or passively marginalize ethnic minorities. Therefore, some minority communities form monoethnic churches because they cannot integrate into the dominant culture.
- Some people from ethnic minorities prefer monocultural churches because these churches create a safe haven from the

1. Lifeway Research, "Protestant Churchgoer Views," 5.
2. DeYoung et al., *United by Faith*.
3. Hardison, "Multi-Ethnic Church Movement," 17.

political opinions and racial biases (and even religious practices) of Christians in the majority culture. In fact, some predominantly Black churches serve as hubs for community organizing and activism.

- Some immigrants prefer monoethnic churches because such churches create opportunities for social and economic networking in a language they understand best.

When I (Ken) was in seminary, I was appointed as a pastor at an entirely White church in a town in Indiana that was over 95 percent White. Even if the church had a vision for racial reconciliation, it would not be able to attain high ethnic diversity. (Note, a monoethnic church that is high in inclusionary vision is described in the advocate posture in chap. 8.) However, the reason the town was over 95 percent White is that it had a long history of overt racism. In fact, during my tenure there in the 1990s, the Ku Klux Klan had rallies in the town, and at one point a cross was burned on someone's lawn. One time, my wife and I invited an ethnically diverse drama team to perform Christian skits at our church, and we needed the congregation to host members of the team overnight. The oldest lady in our congregation seemed to be the most progressive one as well. She told my wife, "I am happy to host any of them. Even the colored lady." While this was jarring to our California-native ears, it felt like a magnanimous gesture on her part. This was a monoethnic, monocultural church in a monoethnic, monocultural town. The first step, in this context, would be to encourage a church like this to move higher in the inclusionary vision domain, thus nudging it toward the advocate posture.

As we mentioned above, not all monoethnic churches have a lack of ethnic diversity for the same reason. Many people prefer to worship in a language and a culture that feel familiar to them, following McGavran's Homogeneous Unit Principle. For instance, although Los Angeles is known for its cultural diversity, pockets of ethnic enclaves continue to exist. Little Tokyo, Chinatown, and Koreatown are areas where some immigrants can operate solely in the languages of their country of heritage, and it is common to find monocultural churches within these enclaves. Throughout my childhood, I (Eunice) attended several monoethnic Korean churches.

These churches weren't necessarily opposed to having non-Koreans attend, but aside from offering simultaneous translation headsets during sermons (generally for the second-generation Koreans who spoke only English), little was done to bridge cultural gaps. Korean immigrant churches served traditional Korean food (especially kimchi) after services and even held Saturday Korean culture classes for children. These classes included morning lessons in the Korean language and afternoon "extracurricular activities," with boys taking Korean martial arts (Tae Kwon do) and girls participating in art or traditional Korean dance.

While there are many good arguments for the "multi-ethnic mandate,"[4] we should avoid the temptation to cast monocultural churches in a negative light. Ian Duncum, Miriam Pepper, Nicole Hancock, and Ruth Powell conducted a fascinating study of over 2,500 Australian churches, comparing vitality indicators between monocultural Anglo churches, monocultural non-English churches, and multicultural churches.[5] The vitality factors included the extent to which they described the worship experience as "inspired," the frequency of engagement in community service, and the cohesiveness of fellowship in the church. In some cases, the monocultural non-English congregations had higher vitality markers than the monocultural Anglo churches or the multicultural churches. Statistically significant differences are listed here:

- Forty-six percent of attendees in monocultural non-English congregations said they "always experienced inspiration in worship compared with 28% of attenders at Anglo churches and 35% of attenders at multicultural churches."
- Fifty-two percent of attendees at monocultural non-English congregations said they had "invited someone to church in the last year, compared with 35% and 27% of attenders at Anglo and multicultural churches respectively."
- Twenty-four percent of attendees at monocultural non-English congregations said they "would certainly follow up a drifter

4. Hardison, "Multi-Ethnic Church Movement," 14.
5. Duncum et al., "Monocultural and Multicultural Churches."

> from church, compared with 9% and 13% of attenders at Anglo and multicultural churches respectively."[6]

However, the monocultural Anglo congregations in this study had statistically significant higher markers of community service. Thirty-one percent of monocultural Anglo church attendees said they "took part regularly in the service activities of their church, compared with 25% of attenders at non-Anglo churches and 24% of attenders at multicultural churches."[7]

It would be overstating the significance of the research done by Duncum and his team to say that monocultural non-Anglo churches are therefore healthier than monocultural Anglo and multicultural churches. However, their study does help debunk the notion that monocultural churches *necessarily* lack vitality in comparison to multicultural churches. A case can be made, theologically, for the multicultural church. But it would be sketchy to argue that multicultural churches are necessarily healthier than monocultural ones (at least using the markers for vitality in their study). Their findings do suggest that non-Anglo churches have strengths—especially in the areas of intimacy in worship and evangelism—that can be a good model for Anglo congregations.

The Difficulties of the Monocultural/Monoethnic Posture

It may seem counterintuitive to suggest that a monocultural or monoethnic church posture presents challenges, yet congregations shaped by a single culture or ethnicity can face significant difficulties. Consider immigrant churches, for example. As second-generation children grow up in the United States, they learn not only the values and traditions of their families' cultures at home but also the language, mannerisms, and social norms of the dominant culture through school, media, and peer relationships. As a result, immigrant churches inevitably face the need to make space for multiple cultures—both the heritage culture that shaped the

6. Duncum et al., "Monocultural and Multicultural Churches," 6.
7. Duncum et al., "Monocultural and Multicultural Churches," 6.

first generation and the surrounding host culture that shapes the lives of the second. This tension often emerges in worship styles, leadership expectations, language use, and theological expression. When churches are unable or unwilling to navigate these dynamics, younger generations may feel caught between two worlds, belonging fully to neither. Over time, this disconnect can lead to disengagement and, ultimately, the loss of the next generation, underscoring the importance of intentional cross-cultural adaptation within immigrant congregations.

In another context, rapidly changing US demographics have made cultural diversity common even in the most remote areas of North America. Communities that were once relatively homogeneous now include people of different ethnicities, languages, and cultural backgrounds, shaped by migration, globalization, and shifting economic patterns. In such settings, it can appear that only deliberate efforts would prevent people of other cultures from joining a congregation—an approach that runs counter to the biblical mandate to love one's neighbor as oneself (Matt. 22:39). Rather than asking how to maintain cultural sameness, churches are increasingly compelled to discern how hospitality, welcome, and discipleship can be practiced across cultural differences. These demographic realities invite congregations to reflect more intentionally on how their cross-cultural posture aligns with both their local context and their theological commitments.

Lastly, while this is not necessarily a difficulty of maintaining a monocultural or monoethnic posture, there is profound beauty and depth in hearing from and learning alongside diverse cultural perspectives. When multiple cultures come together, each contributes its own wisdom, theological insights, and lived experiences, fostering a deeper understanding of both God and one another. As voices from different cultural backgrounds are welcomed and honored, blind spots are revealed, empathy is strengthened, and faith is expressed in richer and more faithful ways. Rather than threatening unity, such diversity deepens it, reflecting the breadth of God's creativity and offering a foretaste of the reconciled community envisioned in Scripture.

First Peter 2:9: A Biblical Example of the Monocultural/ Monoethnic Posture

In the first century, Jewish people who converted to Christianity faced severe persecution in their home country, so many emigrated to find religious freedom elsewhere in the Roman Empire. Due to linguistic and cultural differences that they encountered in places like the Roman province of Asia (modern-day Türkiye), they congregated in ethnic "enclaves." Peter wrote to these Jewish believers "scattered throughout" (1 Pet. 1:1 NIV) to remind them that their ethnic heritage is valuable in that it can point people to Christ. "But you are a chosen race, a royal priesthood, a holy nation, a people for his own possession, that you may proclaim the excellencies of him who called you out of darkness into his marvelous light" (1 Pet. 2:9).

These Jewish Christian emigrants essentially had a monoethnic, monocultural posture as they lived in a foreign culture. Their small house churches did not reflect the ethnic diversity of their neighborhoods. At this point in the church's development, Peter's encouragement was not expressly that they become more diverse but rather that they remain steadfast and set apart, serving as living testimonies of God's holiness and grace: "Beloved, I urge you as sojourners and exiles to abstain from the passions of the flesh, which wage war against your soul. Keep your conduct among the Gentiles honorable, so that when they speak against you as evildoers, they may see your good deeds and glorify God on the day of visitation" (1 Pet. 2:11–12).

Due to massive waves of immigration in recent decades, there are many examples of churches in voluntary or forced exile today. Due to language and cultural differences, newly arrived immigrants often form monocultural church communities. But just as the early Jewish Christian immigrants served as a lighthouse to those around them, these ethnically monocultural churches have found opportunities for "diaspora missions."[8] That is, their immigration gives them the opportunity to reach their own ethnic people who have moved abroad. For example, as Nigerian Christians immigrate to Nigerian enclaves in Western Europe and the United States, they have a unique opportunity to reach Nigerian Muslims for Christ.

8. Galadima and George, *Africans in Diaspora*.

CHAPTER SUMMARY

While there are many compelling arguments in favor of multiethnic churches, it is important to avoid portraying monocultural congregations in a negative light. As noted earlier, monoethnic churches exist for a variety of reasons, and a lack of ethnic diversity does not always reflect exclusion or resistance to change. Many individuals choose to worship in settings where the language and cultural expressions feel familiar and accessible. Moreover, numerous studies suggest that monocultural churches possess distinct strengths, particularly in fostering intimacy in worship and effectiveness in evangelism, making this model well suited to certain congregational contexts.

Things to Watch for with the Monocultural/Monoethnic Posture

- Consider if the choice to remain monocultural is driven by fear of the ethnic Other.
- Ensure that, whether intentional or not, the voices and experiences of ethnic Others are not overlooked.
- Be honest about reasons why the church might be reluctant to change.

A Sunday at The Redemption Church

When I (Eunice) drove up to The Redemption Church on a Sunday morning in the western suburbs of Chicago, I wouldn't have known there was a church there if it hadn't been for nicely dressed Korean American families walking into the corporate building. Because the church meets in a shared office space, the congregation must set up and break down everything each week—including microphones, cables, sound system, projection screens, and even tables and chairs.

As I walked in, I noticed a traveler box of coffee and a small box of donut holes. A few people were enjoying the refreshments before the service began. Just beyond the snack area was a large table, where a banner hung with the church's name and logo. Older youth stood at the table, helping parents check in their children for Sunday school. While everyone was friendly and greeted one another quietly, I noticed there were no ushers or greeters stationed at the entrance.

The service started promptly at 10:30 a.m., led by two guitarists, a vocalist, and a cajón player. While the church's website does not emphasize any specific Asian American identity, I quickly noticed that I was surrounded predominantly by Korean Americans. However, although the congregation was primarily Korean American, the structure and style of the service was not distinctly Korean. In fact, the Sunday service closely resembled that of a typical Anglo evangelical church. Everything was conducted in English, including the children's Sunday school. The children were excused after a time of corporate singing, and they met their Sunday school teachers in the lobby. They rode the elevators together to the second floor and quickly settled into their respective classrooms for Bible study and the day's lesson.

The main service included contemporary worship songs, a time for corporate prayer, announcements, a sermon, a response song, and a closing benediction. Following the benediction, there did not appear to be a designated time for fellowship. People moved quickly to help break down equipment and clean the hallways. At that point, I also made my way out of the office building and back to the parking lot.

The Redemption Church currently operates as a monocultural, multisite church, holding two Sunday services in different locations, but the same pastor preaches at both locations each week. After concluding the first service in the suburbs, he drives to the second location in downtown Chicago to deliver the same message. (Having attended several churches with a similar structure, I've noticed that this is a common pattern among Korean American monocultural, multisite churches. Even when there are different worship teams at each location, it's often the same lead pastor who preaches at both services, even when the campuses are more than thirty minutes apart.)

Another observation that I made of the eight English-speaking, second-generation (or beyond) Korean American churches I visited in both Los Angeles and the Chicago area was that all but one were in temporary locations. Most were borrowing space—meeting in high schools, community centers, corporate buildings, or even art galleries.

Why the Monocultural/Monoethnic Posture Makes Sense for The Redemption Church

Not all Korean American or Asian American churches have a monocultural/monoethnic posture. In fact, as we'll explore later in the book, many Asian American immigrant churches take on a language-group posture, reflecting the presence of multiple languages spoken on any given Sunday.

There are various reasons why immigrant and immigrant-American churches adopt specific ministry models. For example, some churches hold separate Korean and English services each Sunday, typically with first-generation Korean immigrants attending the Korean-speaking service and second-generation Korean Americans attending the English-speaking one. Other churches adopt an interdependent model, characterized by a shared-space posture. In this arrangement, two congregations—one Korean-speaking and one English-speaking—remain independent but share the same campus and resources, meeting either simultaneously or at different times.

In a third model, English-speaking Korean American congregations, like The Redemption Church, plant a fully autonomous church, operating completely independently from the original immigrant church. The members and pastors of these churches are ethnically Korean, but their cultural identity as Korean Americans sets them apart from both Korean immigrant churches and mainstream Anglo churches. As a result, they have pioneered new church plants that specifically serve this unique cultural and generational demographic.

REFLECTION QUESTIONS

1. What factors explain the persistence of monocultural churches today?
2. How should a monocultural church in a largely monocultural town respond to multicultural and multiethnic diversity?
3. What type of church did you grow up in: monocultural or multicultural? What do you think influenced this?

CHAPTER 8

The Advocate Posture

Characteristics of an Advocate Posture

Acts 10:34–48

Strengths:
Demonstrates that people of all ethnicities matter

Weaknesses:
Demonstrating authenticity that the vision is owned by the church

Context:
Region that has experienced interracial tensions

Calling:
To advocate for the marginalized

Constituency:
Largely monocultural group that has a heart for reaching across ethnic/racial lines

Kenneth Nehrbass

Chapter Goals

By the end of this chapter, you should be able to do the following:

- identify obstacles to adopting an advocate posture
- evaluate strategies for incorporating more advocacy strategies in your church

In the advocate posture, the congregation consists predominantly of one ethnicity (over 80 percent), and the worship style remains monocultural. However, the church scores high in inclusionary vision. It is committed to standing in solidarity with people from different cultural backgrounds and works toward racial reconciliation. The church may express a desire for cultural unity, and the pastor may address racial issues in sermons, but despite this commitment, the demographics of the surrounding neighborhood may not yet reflect the diversity that the church seeks. While racial diversity in the congregation may come gradually, the church with an advocate posture has a clear plan to move forward and realize its vision of becoming a multiethnic community.

In many situations, as pastor Angel Cartagena notes, an increase in diversity does not necessarily mean that churches are "either able, or willing, to address the socioeconomic and political disparities existing in our nation. . . . It's often the case that these churches have been unable to resolve these issues within their own walls."[1] However, the advocate posture is one where the church intentionally seeks to address such issues. Hahrie Han describes the experiences of four individuals who attended a church program called Undivided,[2] which equips people to fight against racial injustice: "People in Undivided were willing to risk some of their deepest and most personal relationships to stand up for justice. This course was not scripted by the how-to manuals on antiracism. Instead, it was rooted in a deeply personal commitment to a vision of the world that [the individuals] were desperate to see realized."[3]

1. Cartagena, *Race and the American Church*, 53.
2. Han, *Undivided*. See Undivided, accessed February 7, 2026, https://undivided.us/.
3. Han, *Undivided*, 238.

Advocacy is part of the DNA of Oakhurst Presbyterian Church in Decatur, Georgia. Their passion for interracial reconciliation was chronicled by Nibs Stroupe and Inez Fleming in *While We Run This Race: Confronting the Power of Racism in a Southern Church*.[4] Oakhurst has a Race, Ethnicity, and Diversity team and a peacemaking and justice team that advocates for human rights. The church calendar involves three racial justice vigils a week. The core values specifically reference justice, diversity, and inclusion. The sermons reference human rights and equality. It has high inclusionary vision. However, despite earlier predictions that the church's future would be highly ethnically diverse,[5] currently the church struggles to reach the level of ethnic diversity described in chapter 5.

The advocate posture is more common in Black churches. "The black church, in particular, has always been a bulwark against bigotry. Forged in the fires of racial prejudice, the black church emerged as the ark of safety of people of African descent."[6] A predominantly Black church on the West Coast with an advocate posture is Second Baptist Church in Los Angeles (the first Baptist Church in Los Angeles was predominantly White, so Black Baptists started Second Baptist in 1885). The church raised money for the civil suit *Brown v. Board of Education*; it hosted the NAACP; and it hosted activist pastors such as Al Sharpton, Jesse Jackson, and Martin Luther King Jr.[7] In 2024, Second Baptist Church had programming related to National Slavery and Human Trafficking Prevention Month, and they celebrated Indigenous Peoples' Day, Veteran's Emphasis Day, and Women's Emphasis Day. They sent out information related to California ballot measures and made public statements about presidential candidates. Their church was, of course, an official polling place.

Likewise, Word of Encouragement Community Church in Hawthorne, California, has an advocate posture. Pastor Najuma Smith-Pollard, who balances her ministry with her responsibilities as an assistant director at the USC Center for Religion and Civic Culture, protested along with other church members after

4. Stroupe and Fleming, *While We Run This Race*.
5. Foster, *Embracing Diversity*, 5.
6. Tisby, *The Color of Compromise*, 19.
7. National Park Service, "California: Second Baptist Church."

the death of George Floyd in 2020. She explains the connection between Christianity and community organizing: "My faith informs my activism. It's not a choice. I think that's the case for a lot of people in the Black church. How we do activism might differ. That activism might take place through the arts, through protest, through the pen."[8]

In addition to engaging in activism through protests, the arts, and the pen, Black churches in Los Angeles with the advocate posture have played a prominent role in nonviolent protests. Pastor Cecil "Chip" Murray's First African Methodist Episcopal Church was key in quelling the racially charged riots after the acquittal of police officers in the Rodney King case.[9]

Juan Martínez recounts the journey into activism for his predominantly Latino church:

> We started the peace and justice committee. Through them we joined with an African American church to address the issues of White police officers killing Black citizens. We marched and we protested with them. We continued to address this issue in our church, from the pulpit and in other groups. We addressed how Latinos had been prejudiced against Blacks, in Latin America and in the United States. We worked with a Caribbean preacher in our congregation to develop a conference on the issue, which was presented in our denomination's Latino Bible Institute.[10]

When church members at East Lake Church in Irmo, South Carolina, filled out the Cross-Cultural Posture Assessment Tool, responses were divided about whether the church has reached the level of ethnic diversity necessary for pushing the church from the advocate posture to the reconciling posture. But if I (Ken) can count myself as a tie-breaker, I would say that it is near the tipping point of high ethnic diversity but has not quite reached that level. The images of the church on the website are multiethnic. The senior pastor and the youth pastor are both Black. But the level of diversity on the leadership team (paid

8. Solis et al., "Why Activism Thrives."
9. Solis et al., "Why Activism Thrives."
10. Branson and Martínez, *Churches, Cultures and Leadership*, 77.

and volunteer) is not quite 80 percent, and the church may still be more than 80 percent White in the pews.

However, the church has high inclusionary vision. They regularly hold study groups that go through David Anderson's *Gracism: The Art of Inclusion*[11] as well as a six-part video series on inclusion called "The After Party."[12] The leadership team attended the Multiethnic Church Roundtable at Transformation Church, a gathering for ministry leaders that focuses on building multiethnic communities. And a group from the church recently visited a historical site in South Carolina with an intact slave market, where they prayed and lamented the sin of racism. Michelle Trayers, discipleship pastor at East Lake, said, "We do a lot to try to help people understand that their allegiance should not be to anyone but King Jesus first. And so I think that helps in making African American people comfortable."

Martin, an African American, and his wife Valeria, a first-generation Ecuadorian, are "gracism" coaches at East Lake.[13] They decided to become active members at East Lake because of its advocacy posture. Martin told us,

> One of the main reasons why we decided to stay at the church was because East Lake wasn't afraid of having the tough discussions, the tough conversations from the front. It's one thing for small groups to potentially have those discussions, but it's a whole other thing whenever the leadership themselves are actually having those discussions about what's going on in our community and in our world. And so we've been able to really deal with those situations; just understanding where they're coming from has been very valuable for us to be in that community.

For example, Martin appreciates that during Black History Month, Pastor Rob, who is White, shared "the hate or the slurs that were used in his family and how he was even one of those individuals that used them, and how God had changed his heart. And you know, he has an adopted son now who is African American. And he has to remind families and friends of certain things."

11. Anderson, *Gracism*.
12. Redeeming Babel, "The After Party."
13. See Gracism Global, accessed February 7, 2026, https://gracismglobal.com/.

The Difficulties of the Advocate Posture

In one of our focus groups, we interviewed members of a church that was highly intentional about addressing reconciliation and injustice. However, participants expressed confusion and even some frustration over the lack of participation from people of color, noting that only Anglo American members were actively involved in the ministries aimed at bridging cultural divides. Carrie shared, "The people of the church who are most involved are a lot of the White people. I feel like they feel like the main body. . . . We're starting to get some regulars from the neighborhood and others who are people of color, but I think it definitely feels like a White church at its core, even if we don't want to be. We have this mission, but we're definitely not perfect about it."

Doris agreed, saying that it seems that while their church is open to welcoming people, the act of inclusion requires a different type of approach: "Mostly White people are doing the service stuff within the church, but there are people of color teaching and on the platform. . . . One of the things that I'm really concerned about is the difference between welcome and inclusion. Welcome is 'you may come here and join us in what we're doing,' and inclusion is 'I recognize that I will be influenced by you. I will be changed by you. And the way we do things will change because we have known you and welcomed you, and we care that you have an experience that we have.'"

Lonnie, a Latin American from the same congregation, shared that being involved in various committees often makes her feel like the token:

> The racial reconciliation committee is mostly White people and some African American presence. But it's interesting that in the diversity, inclusion, and equity committee, I'm the only woman of color. I'm not saying that's horrible, terrible, but the planning is done mostly by White people, which on the one hand, if you have White people telling other White people, that's their responsibility. Sometimes people of color, we become tokens, and we become the voice and it becomes my responsibility. . . . I live with having to be the token, I have to deal with that in my every decision, and then

> on top of that, having to expose myself and be vulnerable even at church. So a lot of times, communities of color tend to be a little bit more guarded.

Similarly, at another church, a focus group discussed the challenge of self-segregation within the church and commented on the need for more intentional mixing. For instance, they noted that although the church had intentionally organized monthly lunch fellowships after the service, people still tended to sit separately. Or, in another example, one church member noted that when someone hosted a ladies' brunch at her house, "All the Asian-looking people were talking at one side of the person's house and all of the White-looking people were over on the other side. I was like, 'Well, that's interesting.' You know, people still flocked to those with similarities."

Moreover, at another church across the country, a few participants shared about an annual conference that their church hosts every year on the topic of racial equity. One person said,

> Our church might not be the right place for you if you're not ready to have these kinds of discussions. When we first started having these conferences, it was very much topics on "What is White privilege?" and "Does systemic racism exist?" . . . Over the years it has shifted to faith, race, and immigration and faith, race, and education. Going deeper into those things, assuming that people have done that basic work. It does put off some people if they're coming into the place where they haven't done that work yet. Everyone's in a different place in their journey, and this may not be the place for you to enter in. We welcome you, however, if you want to enter in.

Participants in our interviews also mentioned instances where church attendees walked out, upset that the church would even host such conversations. For instance, they recalled that an Anglo woman once exclaimed that she was tired of being told "It's your fault." In response, the pastor said, "If you want to talk about this more, I will get in touch with you, but we're going to make this a space for everybody." The pastor's intentional effort to create a safe space for everyone gave the participants a sense of unity, prompting the feeling of "Yep, we are one community."

Additionally, in this model the debate about whether the church should prioritize the gospel over social justice issues may become more pronounced. As the church engages with matters of injustice, some may feel that the emphasis shifts away from the gospel and toward social concerns. During an interview, one pastor said, "If we're not careful in seeking Jesus, justice is simply vengeance and the oppressed becomes the oppressor. And so we really need to be careful." As Mae Elise Cannon states, "Various methodologies are offered to solve systemic injustice and to provoke effective change. . . . However, material change is not enough. Change must go deeper. It must happen on a spiritual level. Lasting and effective change comes when the soul is transformed and true community is pursued."[14]

Acts 10:34–48: A Biblical Example of the Advocate Posture

It took a vision from heaven (actually, three of them) for Peter to break out of his bubble and become an advocate for the inclusion of all ethnic groups. As a Jew in the ancient Near East, Peter had learned that his people belonged to a privileged race. In fact, strict laws separated the races so that they could not even drink at the same water fountain, let alone worship together in the same place. But God shattered this exclusionary approach for Peter by giving him a vision. A sheet with non-kosher animals (such as lobster, swine, and catfish) came down from heaven, and God told Peter, "Rise, Peter; kill and eat" (Acts 10:13). Peter had a religious justification for refusing the foods that were "unclean." But the voice in the vision said, "Do not call anything impure that God has made clean" (Acts 10:15 NIV).

At first, Peter could not figure out the meaning of the vision, but then Cornelius, a non-Jewish man, invited Peter into his home. Then Peter understood the vision. He explained his paradigm shift: "Truly I understand that God shows no partiality, but in every nation anyone who fears him and does what is right is acceptable to him" (Acts 10:34–35). Peter explained the gospel to Cornelius, and the whole

14. Cannon, *Social Justice Handbook*, 106.

family converted. Peter then invited them into God's family with the visible act of water baptism. "[The Jewish believers and] Peter were amazed, because the gift of the Holy Spirit was poured out even on the Gentiles" (Acts 10:45).

Remember, at this point the early church was primarily monoethnic. It was composed of Jewish followers of Jesus, and their worship practices were still rooted in their Jewish heritage (e.g., circumcision, food laws, worship in the temple). But the church in Jerusalem was beginning to advocate for the inclusion of people from all ethnic groups. And this advocacy was no less polarizing or costly for the church than it is today. The reason why Jewish people took "offense at the gospel" was not only that Paul preached the death and resurrection of Jesus Christ—though the Sadducees took issue with this (Acts 23:8)—but also that Paul insisted that God had opened the door for all people groups to worship God without having to follow Jewish customs (Acts 13:47–48; 18:5–6). This inclusionary vision led to riots, and eventually the Jewish leaders had Paul arrested and planned to ambush Paul and kill him (Acts 23:12–35).

Similarly, churches with an advocate posture are composed predominantly of people from one ethnicity and cultural background. These churches have a strong commitment to racial and cultural unity and are ready to embrace and welcome those from different ethnic backgrounds, but they have not yet achieved the momentum necessary for becoming ethnically diverse. Again, this sort of inclusionary vision can be polarizing even today. But churches with the advocate posture are up for the task in part because of the biblical example set by Peter and Paul.

CHAPTER SUMMARY

A church with an advocate posture is one that maintains a strong inclusionary vision but has not yet attained a high level of ethnic diversity. For these churches, being the church and standing with the marginalized are inseparable concepts: To follow Jesus is to care about the foreigner or sojourner in our midst and to walk with the oppressed. Interestingly, though, churches' stances on advocacy can cause division (especially along political lines). Churches should consider how a plurality of voices can be included in the pursuit of biblically grounded advocacy.

Things to Watch for with the Advocate Posture

- Persevere even if the congregation's demographics do not yet align with the church's vision and/or desire to be multiethnic.
- Maintain a gospel-centered focus while being mindful of differing opinions, especially in the context of societal pressures surrounding polarizing issues.

A Sunday at East Lake Community Church

I (Ken) pull into a parking lot located at the edge of where the metropolitan Columbia area starts to become rural. I enter the warehouse-style building of East Lake Community Church in Irmo, South Carolina, and notice that the mission statement of the church is prominently displayed at the entrance to the auditorium: "As an intentional multicultural community, empowered by the Holy Spirit, we will passionately pursue a loving relationship with God, and those he sent Jesus to die for here, near, and far."

There is also wood art on the wall; one is a map of Africa, and another of Mexico. I hear the song "Júbilo" ["Jubilee"][a] playing on the sound system as the time nears for the service to begin. It is the only example of multilingualism I notice during the day, except for the multigenerational family that sits in front of me, speaking Spanish.

The 250 seats in the auditorium are mostly full when the service starts at exactly 9:00 a.m., and the worship team leads the congregation in three contemporary Christian songs. Some may have noticed that one of the songs was a remake of the 1875 hymn "Man of Sorrows" by P. P. Bliss.

Pastor Ray Washington makes some announcements. Then Pastor Rob Townsend continues the preaching series through the book of Mark. I scroll through the church's archives and notice that Pastor Ray preaches about 40 percent of the time and Pastor Michelle and Pastor Rob each preach about 25 percent of the Sundays, with the remaining Sundays filled by others in the church or by guest preachers. All three teaching pastors have similar preaching styles: a mix of narrative, expository, and emotional plea.

There is an offering, a benediction, and an offer for prayer. Many file out to collect their children from the children's programs; others get a drink from the coffee bar and socialize—staying and chatting, even as the 11:00 a.m. service starts.

Why the Advocate Posture Makes Sense for East Lake

The metropolitan area of Columbia, South Carolina, is 71 percent White and 18 percent Black, with a painful past when it comes to interracial relations. East Lake Church does not quite reach that level of ethnic diversity. However, I get the impression that the church is more diverse than the Black and predominantly White churches in the area. East Lake has been highly intentional about integration.

Angel Cartagena surmises, "Most multiracial congregations have a White pastor, because most Whites cannot see themselves submitting to the authority of a Black pastor."[b] Either East Lake has challenged this assertion or East Lake is an outlier. Regardless, East Lake is located in a part of the country with a troubled history of racism that continues to hurt Black and White relationships. East Lake, a majority White congregation, follows the lead of a Black pastor who can help them embrace the biblical role of advocacy.

a. Maverick City Music, "Júbilo," accessed February 7, 2026, https://maverickcitymusic.com/.
b. Cartagena, *Race and the American Church*, 53.

REFLECTION QUESTIONS

1. What topics of racial reconciliation would your church be willing to address? What topics would be considered "off-limits"?
2. Why are churches uniquely positioned to address racial reconciliation?
3. If your church has an advocate posture, what changes could be made to move it toward a reconciling posture (i.e., a posture that has high inclusionary vision and high ethnic diversity)?

CHAPTER 9

The Multiethnic Posture

Characteristics of a Multiethnic Posture

Acts 6:1–7

Strengths:
Demonstrates people of all ethnicities have a place

Weaknesses:
Can create a monoculture; “colorblind”

Context:
High ethnic diversity; second generation and beyond

Calling:
To reach all people in the neighborhood

Constituency:
English speaking; ethnically diverse

Kenneth Nehrbass

Chapter Goals

By the end of this chapter, you should be able to do the following:

- describe and evaluate your church's ethnic "mix"
- identify how some churches have become highly ethnically diverse

In a multiethnic posture, the congregation consists of individuals from various ethnic backgrounds, reflecting the diversity of the community. However, church life does not incorporate multiple languages or various cultural styles in the programming and leadership. True, this posture at times may lean toward assimilation, as Safwat Marzouk has pointed out,[1] but it is not necessarily a forced assimilation. Numerous leaders in the multicultural church movement have noticed that second- and third-generation immigrants have assimilated to the extent that they feel uncomfortable in the ethnic churches of their parents.[2] They may not even speak the language of their parents' first-generation Chinese, Hispanic, or Korean churches. They also clash with the leadership values of their ethnic churches, as they have adopted American values of egalitarianism and individualism, and prefer the worship style found in the majority culture.

Because they have adopted or "owned" majority culture to this extent, the contemporary monocultural worship experience is as much *second- and third-generation immigrant* culture as it is *Anglo* culture.

Humberto, the son of immigrants from South America, speaks Spanish, but his wife and children do not. He and his wife chose to become active at a multiethnic church in Southern California. He felt that the Spanish-speaking "strict" Apostolic church was his "parents' church." He and his wife wanted a nondenominational English-speaking church with a strong children's program. While his church is highly ethnically diverse, we wondered if the lack of multiculturality bothered him. He told us, "I'm American, and I don't feel left out because I live in America and I am American. And

1. Marzouk, *Intercultural Church*, 4.
2. Edwards and Kim, *Estranged Pioneers*, 82; Hearn, *Technicolor*, 12.

so I don't need to feel 'represented.' God represents me. That's really what matters—that God's there in our church—not that my parents' native land is represented."

A bit later Humberto reflected on attempts at higher levels of multiculturality at his church: "I mean, sometimes they'll throw in half a song in Spanish, and that's cool. It kind of wakes me up a little bit. I would like to see that a little more, but it's not necessary. It's not going to make me leave my church or anything like that."

Gerardo Martí describes this phenomenon at Mosaic in Los Angeles: "Mosaic provides a haven for second and third generation ethnics escaping from mono-ethnic home churches. While their parents and grandparents have often been part of a monoethnic, immigrant church, they feel they do not 'fit.' They chafe against the demand to be not just respectful but representative of their ancestral culture. Yet within the broadly Americanized culture of Mosaic, they find refuge for 'being' ethnic without having to 'act' ethnic."[3] Martí also reported that White people appreciate the diversity of Mosaic Los Angeles because they are confident that when they invite their friends of color, they won't feel out of place.[4]

Alyssa, whose family is from Egypt, described the importance of "representation" at The Grove Community Church: "It's why I love The Grove so much, just being able to see so many different people represented. Not just on the worship team, but our pastors, all of that. It made me feel like I was at home. . . . We went to Wisconsin for Christmas . . . and we did go to a church out there that was probably 99 percent Anglo. And I did not enjoy it. I don't know, I can't quite place how I felt."

Given that three-quarters of churches are not multiethnic, how do churches pull off this feat? George Yancey delineates four ways that churches become multiethnic:[5]

1. The main pastor has a persona that draws people from different ethnic groups.
2. The church reflects demographic changes in the neighborhood.

3. Martí, "Mosaic on Mission," 89.
4. Martí, "Mosaic on Mission," 159.
5. Yancey, *One Body, One Spirit*.

3. There are deliberate evangelistic efforts among various ethnic groups.
4. People with multiethnic relationships bring their friends to church.

Centerpoint Church in Colton, California, is a good example of a church with a multiethnic posture. The website reveals that people from Hispanic, Asian, and White backgrounds worship together, and the worship team and leadership team are racially diverse. There is no overt commitment to racial diversity, and the programming does not expressly target racial reconciliation. However, there is clear oneness and togetherness. The diverse congregation worships, fellowships, serves, and grows together.

Another example of a church with a multiethnic posture is Living Stones Church in Kona, Hawaii. Like Centerpoint, Living Stones is ethnically diverse. However, its website does not explicitly mention a commitment to racial reconciliation. According to members of the congregation, Hawaii's natural ethnic diversity is deeply ingrained in the local culture, and the church simply reflects the demographics of the surrounding community.

Many people of color and those in interracial marriages find belonging in attending a multiethnic church. For instance, Melina and her family had always desired to attend a multiethnic church like the one they're part of now, as their own family is multiethnic. In an interview, Melina shared that when her cousin invited her to a monocultural church, she felt extremely awkward and out of place.

> My cousin invited us to a different church. It was a stark difference because that's when I truly realized how Sunday is by far the most segregated day in America, especially in the South. I walked in there, and I tell you, all eyes were on me, and I was the lightest thing in that room. But it wasn't an inviting look, it was, "Oh, you stand out." "You are different." Nobody came to us at the end of the service to introduce themselves. Nothing. . . . We came, we took up a seat, and we left. And at that moment I thought, "We are a multicultural family. Our children need to grow up seeing this as well." . . . So at home I only speak Spanish to my children. My husband only speaks French

> to our children. We're not this cultural piece; this is our ethnicity. So coming to our current church, we're able to embody that, like fully embody that and fully live into that. . . . So it's just trying to create, really integrate ourselves and have our children grow up in an environment that can resemble heaven as closely as possible.

Daniel shared a similar experience:

> I grew up in a multiracial family but in a very segregated place during the civil rights era, in a predominantly Black church. Even though you may have been part of a multiracial family in that era, you were Black. That's the camp you were put in. And so growing up in a predominantly Black church during that era had a lot of racial overtones. That's how I was raised. I mean, I was very grounded in faith. And my family, particularly my maternal side, was very active in the church growing up. And it was all good, but fast-forward. My wife is White, we have an interracial marriage, and she grew up in a predominantly White church. As our marriage progressed and we started having kids, it was very clear to us that we could not find a place where either one of us felt comfortable. We would actually take turns. We would go to a predominantly Black church, and she would feel out of place, and we would go to a White church, and I would feel out of place, but I was used to that. You know, all the eyes go on you when you're the odd person out.

Daniel started joining his current church's service online during the height of the COVID restrictions. As he became more involved, he realized that a different way to worship was available for his family: "I have been to many churches throughout the country because I've had to move around so much, but I have never been to a church like this—that is truly gospel-centered, welcoming, and reflects God's intent for his family. It's amazing. It's been a beautiful experience."

Daniel went on to share that he eventually invited his friend, who also came to check out the multiethnic church:

> One of the things that just really just warmed my heart, which I think just speaks volumes about this place, . . . there was this young man and his family, who were from Liberia, and they felt very out of place at their previous church. So when I came here, I told them about this place, and

> he decided to come and visit. He and his wife came and visited, and he could not wait to come and see me after the service was over. And I asked him, "What do you think?" And he said, "I walked in and nobody looked at me. . . . I just sat down and it's like everybody around me was like me." It just warmed my heart, and it was just a beautiful thing.

The Difficulties of a Multiethnic Posture

While a church may have a high level of ethnic diversity, it may not have an explicit commitment to racial reconciliation. Yancey notes that churches sometimes become ethnically diverse due to demographic shifts such as "White flight," or the establishment of immigrant communities within a city.[6]

Based on a qualitative study, Korie Little Edwards and Rebecca Kim theorized that the only way multiethnic churches can survive in a predominantly White city is to adopt a monocultural style—one that represents White middle-class culture.[7] According to them, this typically includes staying out of identity politics.[8] What's interesting is that people of color at the multiethnic churches in our study also evidenced a sort of "colorblind" ideology. For example, Humberto, a second-generation immigrant, was leery about focusing on ethnic diversity: "I think only some people see color as an obstacle. But I can't recall any problems. I remember somebody telling me, 'Oh, this is a White church.' I'm like, 'Well, I mean, it kind of is a majority, but there are still a lot of other ethnicities that come here.' So I never saw anything where the church actually did something to prevent anybody from doing anything, just based on their skin color or anything."

Linda, the granddaughter of immigrants from Mexico, worships at the same church as Humberto. She also held this colorblind philosophy:

> I feel like my culture does not have to be represented here. Or actually, I don't think anywhere I go I have to see my culture represented.

6. Yancey, *One Body, One Spirit*.
7. Edwards and Kim, *Estranged Pioneers*, 78.
8. Edwards and Kim, *Estranged Pioneers*, 79.

> I don't feel the church should be geared toward any one ethnicity or culture. It's more the ground base of "this is about Christ." It's about the message of Scripture. . . . If I want my culture represented, that would be up to me. If I were to come in a huipil dress or something. I know I would still be welcomed if I want to have this big Mexican dress with flowers in my hair—which is beautiful—but it's not necessary. I know that I would feel the freedom to do that.

Both Humberto and Linda were far more passionate about describing how their church has helped them understand Scripture—and have a relationship with Christ—than they were about discussing the cross-cultural posture of the church. Sandra, whose parents emigrated from Mexico, also has a colorblind philosophy about the sermons:

> I think that every message speaks to all of us, I don't necessarily think that they have to address issues to make it relevant, because we're all different, but so similar. We're all dealing with the same thing. We're all dealing with the same issues. Like as parents, we're all dealing with the same issues with our children. . . . They're preaching the Word and they're keeping it very straightforward, that's it. Just the Word. We're not mixing anything else. We're just preaching the Word, and I think that's why it reaches so many different people.

While some multiculturalists would take issue with a colorblind approach, Sandra, Linda, and Humberto have highlighted that many in the pews—at least those in churches with multiethnic postures—do tend toward the colorblind approach.

Mark Branson and Juan Martínez echo a commonly held belief that those multiethnic churches that do not expressly seek ethnic or cultural inclusivity inevitably "tend to exhibit the dominance of one culture, leaving others to lack full agency because they are aware that they will always be guests."[9] In an interview on NPR, Keith Moore, a pastor in Montgomery, Alabama, described his own experience of fostering a heterogeneous church: "You have to abandon some

9. Branson and Martínez, *Churches, Cultures and Leadership*, 8.

of your ethnic culture and become more palatable to the majority-White culture, give up some of the old traditional African American experience to fit in. So there is a sacrifice."[10] Or as sociologists Brad Christerson, Korie Little Edwards, and Michael Emerson note, "It is one thing to allow Spanish speakers to enjoy a song or two in their language and to hear the sermon in Spanish, but quite another to integrate them fully into the leadership and social life of the church."[11]

Because of these previous empirical studies, we really wanted to know if people from various ethnic backgrounds who attend multi-ethnic (but not multicultural) churches "miss" the representation of their ancestral culture. Do they feel that the worship music is "White," and if so, is that a problem for them? However, interestingly, none of the interviewees at our multiethnic churches expressed a feeling that the worship environment was White-normative. We did not encounter anyone who referred to "White worship music" or a "White preaching style" or a "White leadership style." Interviewees referred to "Bethel style,"[12] "Hillsong-typical,"[13] "Elevation style,"[14] or "Phil Wickham,"[15] but did not overtly relate worship styles to race or ethnicity. And some push against that notion. For example, Humberto said, "It's Christian music. It's God's. That's how I see it, it's God's music. Do I like some music better than others? Yeah, I lean more toward Phil Wickham–type of music, I guess. And you know, what's the other—the guy who married a Cuban lady—Danny Gokey."

However, Humberto's senior pastor is attuned to the possibility that different worship styles may represent different cultural backgrounds. Nonetheless, like other participants, he finds it easier to identify worship bands by name than to refer to "Latino worship" or "Black worship" styles:

> We went to a conference several years ago . . . and it was one of the greatest worship services we'd ever been to. The church was a

10. Gjelton, "Multiracial Congregations."
11. Christerson, Edwards, and Emerson, *Against All Odds*, 93.
12. Bethel Music, accessed February 7, 2026, https://bethelmusic.com/.
13. Hillsong Music, accessed February 7, 2026, https://hillsong.com/music/.
14. Elevation Worship, accessed February, 7, 2026, https://www.elevationworship.com/.
15. Phil Wickham, accessed February 7, 2026, https://philwickham.com/.

> Black church, that's the church that was hosting the event, and it was just so much fun. Took me back to when I was a kid, because that's how I grew up in a Hispanic church. Lots of energy. . . . So as we're leaving, our worship pastor, who was with us, says, "I'm just gonna say it: White music is boring." And he's as White as they come. And so we all kind of laughed about it, and I told them, "I've been trying to tell you guys all of our music, there are no highs, there are no energy moments. It's just, you know, kind of swaying that gets boring after a minute." We have since introduced more songs that offer something of a gospel feel. What's the name of the band? Rend Collective.[16] They were an older band, but we brought back some of their stuff that offers a lot more energy and excitement. . . . We're trying to get away from the very mellow Bethel style music that is just very flat. . . . But some of the stuff that we've started to introduce now, it offers those high points, those energy points, and I think it's been helpful for our church. Our church loves the worship element. . . . And so we've tried to get away from just a very mellow style, very synth-driven worship.

We learned that for many second- and third-generation descendants of immigrants to the United States, the nondenominational worship experience is more appealing than the cultural and religious traditions of their grandparents. One participant, for example, deliberately left the Orthodox tradition of her parents' church so that she could have a worship experience that used musical styles more familiar to her. In another instance, a Hispanic woman said she deliberately left her parents' Catholic tradition for a more contemporary (she did not say "White") worship experience.

Regardless, some empirical studies suggest that the multiethnic posture comes with some costs. First, ethnic diversity can result in ethnic cliques.[17] While there is high togetherness, there still is not ethnic cohesiveness. Humberto could recall an instance of tension in his small group: "We do have, of course, White and Black in our small group, right? And sometimes they'll say some comments, and they're kind of offensive. But this probably happened one time, and

16. Rend Collective, accessed February 7, 2026, https://rendcollective.com/.
17. Christerson, Edwards, and Emerson, *Against All Odds*.

I didn't notice it, but somebody else did, and I was like, 'Oh, okay, all right. Well, if it continues, then we could address it.'"

Additionally, according to Korie Little Edwards's study of multiethnic churches, racial diversity can result in White hegemony. "For interracial churches to stay interracial, racial minorities must be willing to sacrifice their preferences, or they must have already sufficiently acculturated into and accepted the dominant culture and whites' privileged status."[18] Sometimes these churches integrate minority ethnic groups only to the extent that White people are comfortable with.[19] As Christerson, Edwards, and Emerson observe, when the ethnic diversity becomes uncomfortable, White people tend to feel like they have "lost their church," and they leave the congregation. "Keeping the white constituency committed to the church [is] a key obstacle to maintaining diversity."[20] Angel Cartagena also observes that a "fact that undermines the efficacy of multiethnic churches is that Whites in those churches are often willing to remain so long as the addition of other racial-ethnic groups does not lead to any cultural changes in the church or church service."[21]

A pastor of a large multiethnic church related a story to us about the tensions caused by increasing cultural representation in the church service.

> It was right around the time when all the Syrian refugees were working their way over to the United States. And we sang a song that says, "We want to be a place where freedom rings." Anyway, it mentioned something about refugees, and one of the girls said to me, "I really like that song, but sometimes I'm not convinced that our church is representative of that." And I was like, "Really?" And it had to have been the Holy Spirit or something just to get our attention, because on the other side of the curtain onstage, we heard two guys having a conversation, and one said, "I'm glad we didn't sing a Spanish song today. This is America; we don't need to sing Spanish songs." And me and this girl were standing there, and we're looking at each other because we both heard it, and I was like, "I'm glad I didn't look to

18. Edwards, *The Elusive Dream*, 139.
19. Edwards, *The Elusive Dream*, 6.
20. Christerson, Edwards, and Emerson, *Against All Odds*, 100.
21. Cartagena, *Race and the American Church*, 54.

see who it was, because I don't know how my heart would have been toward that person." It was a hurtful thing to say.

One additional danger of the multiethnic posture is that it may cause churches to feel they have obviated the need to address racial issues. Achieving diversity is remarkable, but it is only a step in addressing racial issues. Jessica Barron and Rhys Williams spent eighteen months studying people's experiences in a church with a multiethnic posture in downtown Chicago. The church was planted by a predominantly White megachurch located in a suburban area about two hours away, and while the leadership team planned, from the start, to be multiethnic, its vision never included topics of racial injustice or reconciliation. They carefully avoided "racialized texts" or messaging.[22] Barron and Williams refer to this approach as "raceless diversity"[23] or "managed diversity."[24] The ethnic diversity in the church was seen by critics in the community as a "racial utility" for protecting the church's brand as a "relevant" church in an urban setting that advances an "urban, but non-black, religious identity."[25]

When Nancy Wadsworth carried out a case study of a multiethnic church in Denver, she concluded that evangelicals aspire to be "faithful to what they see as New Testament principles honoring difference and diversity within the Body of Christ, and to influence the world in turn. But they are not sure that politics, as an individual or a coordinated collective response to race-related problems, is an appropriate expression of that conviction, even outside the church."[26]

One pastor recounted to Edwards that he could promote diversity in his church, but there was an unspoken contract: "Don't talk about race, racism, or racial injustice, and do not talk about white

22. Barron and Williams, *The Urban Church Imagined*.
23. Barron and Williams, *The Urban Church Imagined*, 86.
24. Barron and Williams, *The Urban Church Imagined*, 20.
25. Barron and Williams, *The Urban Church Imagined*, 46.
26. Wadsworth, *Ambivalent Miracles*, 1.

supremacy."[27] Thankfully, the multiethnic church in Acts 6 tackled such inequality head-on.

Acts 6:1–7: A Biblical Example of the Multiethnic Posture

The multiethnic posture reflects the church's approach to believers of various ethnicities in Acts 6. The early church in Jerusalem reflected the diversity of the city but maintained a monocultural worship experience. The city of Jerusalem was known to be a cultural hub, as it was highly diverse. The city not only had a large Jewish population that included both native Israelites and Jews from the Diaspora but also was under significant Greco-Roman cultural influence. In Acts 6, we see two distinct groups in the church in Jerusalem: Hellenistic Jews (Greek-speaking Jews from outside of Jerusalem) and Hebraic Jews (Aramaic-speaking Jews from Jerusalem).

> Now in these days when the disciples were increasing in number, a complaint by the Hellenists arose against the Hebrews because their widows were being neglected in the daily distribution. And the twelve summoned the full number of the disciples and said, "It is not right that we should give up preaching the word of God to serve tables. Therefore, brothers, pick out from among you seven men of good repute, full of the Spirit and of wisdom, whom we will appoint to this duty. But we will devote ourselves to prayer and to the ministry of the word." . . . And the word of God continued to increase, and the number of the disciples multiplied greatly in Jerusalem, and a great many of the priests became obedient to the faith. (Acts 6:1–4, 7)

This passage brings to light some of the tensions the early church had to overcome, but we would like to focus our attention on the fact that although both groups shared the same faith and worshiped together, they were of two very different cultural backgrounds: Greek and Jewish. And while various cultural groups were represented in the early church, at this point the church in Jerusalem was monocultural. It was based on Jewish customs and traditions.

27. Edwards, "The Multiethnic Church."

Similarly, a church with the multiethnic posture reflects multiple nations or ethnic backgrounds, and while the church may include people from all cultural backgrounds, the worship experience is still homogeneous—usually reflecting the majority culture. In most cases, this implies that minority groups assimilate to the majority culture's language and worship style. Important to keep in mind, however, is that the church in Acts 6 had to be alerted to ways it was marginalizing the ethnic minorities. As a result, the church took conscious steps to meet everyone's needs.

CHAPTER SUMMARY

A church with a multiethnic posture scores high in ethnic diversity and oneness but low in multiculturality and inclusionary vision. However, the absence of representation of multiple cultures is not inherently negative. For example, individuals from various ethnic backgrounds who speak only English often prefer to attend worship services in that language. Many people who attend multiethnic churches are second- and third-generation immigrants, and they identify with majority-culture worship music, preaching styles, and leadership styles. There is, however, a danger to watch out for: Churches that are multiethnic but monocultural must be careful to avoid tokenism and ensure that the voices of all ethnic groups in the church are heard. Churches with a multiethnic posture should consider how they can more actively become advocates of racial reconciliation.

Things to Watch for with the Multiethnic Posture

- Ensure that diversity is not just a "tool" for being relevant.
- Consider how the church can protect minority voices from White hegemony.
- As a church, consider how you can guard against racial cliques.
- Gather voices across the ethnic groups to see how you can address racial issues as a church.

A Sunday at Centerpoint Church Colton

I (Ken) park on one of the narrow streets and notice three unhoused individuals sleeping in Veterans Park. I walk across the street and approach the historic building that abuts the sidewalk on two sides. I note that the plaque on the cornerstone indicates that the church was called First Baptist Colton before changing its name to Centerpoint. I notice children funneling into the basement for the children's program as I enter the sanctuary (built in 1887). It retains some of the aura of the historic downtown churches that are found in most of America's midsize cities, but a twelve-foot projection screen hangs in front of organ pipes that likely were played until the end of the twentieth century. Remote-controlled blinds occlude the stained-glass windows during the worship set. And the pews have been replaced by upholstered, removable chairs.

The worship band leads us in three contemporary Christian music songs. I take note that the worship band is composed of young Asian Americans, Blacks, Latinos, and Anglos. I look around the three-hundred-seat sanctuary and notice the same level of diversity, and I think to myself, "If someone grew up in this church, they would be surprised to learn that most of America's churches are racially divided."

The lead pastor, Josué Zapata, preaches a five-point sermon on 1 John 5. We have Communion and an altar call. As I leave the church, I walk the halls and notice images of the church that represent the diversity of the congregation.

Why the Multiethnic Posture Makes Sense for Centerpoint

Although there is high ethnic diversity in Centerpoint Church Colton, they found out that it doesn't make sense to incorporate high multiculturality, because the church attracts primarily descendants of Asian and Latino immigrants who have been in Southern California for two or more generations. In reference to Rick Warren's target audience, "Saddleback Sam" (a middle-aged White professional), leaders at Centerpoint half-jokingly explain that their church reaches "Colton Carlos"—a twenty-nine-year-old Hispanic male who is integrated into majority US culture and may work on Sunday mornings. He expects coffee and donuts in the foyer, not *pan dulce*. Pastor Josué said, "We have done taco carts, but we've also done barbecues." The church offers evening services for the "Colton Carloses" who can't come on Sunday morning. Jeff Keneaster, pastor of care and communication at Centerpoint, added, "A big thing that Colton Carlos really enjoys is something for the family. . . . We encourage the families to come together as a unit. So whether that's grandma and grandson, mom, dad, you know, and brother and sister, they come together as well."

The church used to offer Spanish translation, as the lead pastor explained, "for that grandma that was coming with the family who didn't speak English. . . . We ended up with more translators than those who needed the translation." Yet low multilingualism does not mean *no* multilingualism. As a church member explained, the church has "a couple of small groups that meet and speak Spanish. . . . One that actually meets over Zoom, and then we have a Spanish Wednesday Bible study. And then there's a Spanish women's group that meets seasonally."

Additionally, the church represents the diversity of the city. Humberto added some nuance to the concept of "haven" when he explained that the multiethnic church fits his socioeconomic status: "Colton is not a high-end city. . . . We exactly fit our environment. And I think maybe I don't know if most churches kind of do that. I'm not sure, but yeah, we just feel really at home there."

REFLECTION QUESTIONS

1. How do certain churches become highly ethnically diverse?
2. What is the story of how your church attained the ethnic mix currently represented there?
3. How can your church better serve people of different ethnic communities in the surrounding towns and neighborhoods?

CHAPTER 10

The Language-Group Posture

Characteristics of a Language-Group Posture

Acts 15:1–32

Strengths:
Structure for second-generation speakers; reaches across cultures

Weaknesses:
Low cohesion for those of different language groups

Context:
Town with at least two languages widely spoken; immigrant communities with English-speaking children

Calling:
To reach the community in the languages they know best

Constituency:
A heart for cross-cultural outreach

Kenneth Nehrbass

Chapter Goals

By the end of this chapter, you should be able to do the following:

- explain why some churches may have separate services for speakers of other languages
- identify how your church could extend its reach to speakers of other languages

A church with a language-group posture holds multiple worship services in different languages and styles but has one leadership team, one vision, one budget, and one calendar and communication channel. Keith Watkins used the term "multi-language congregation" to capture this posture,[1] and Rodney Harrison, Tom Cheyney, and Don Overstreet refer to this posture as the multicultural, multilingual model.[2] Churches often have their own way to describe how they accommodate various languages. Some refer to a "Spanish fellowship" or an "English ministry" or a "Vietnamese congregation." Regardless, it is the high oneness that distinguishes this approach from the shared-space model.

Without the development of theoretical categories of togetherness and oneness, scholars have often conflated the shared-space and language-group postures. Manuel Ortiz notes that Peter Wagner, an early leader of the church-growth movement, lumped all multilingual churches into the category "multicongregational." This category includes some that "simply share facilities with ethnic congregations that maintain their own autonomy, while others go so far as to share the entire church administration equitably."[3] And Hyun Choi describes a "multi-congregational" church as one that "comprises culturally diverse communities with monocultural and monoethnic fellowship because language differences pose a barrier

1. Watkins, "Multi-Language Congregations."

2. Harrison, Cheyney, and Overstreet, *Spin-Off Churches*, 77–78.

3. Ortiz, *One New People*, 64. Ortiz further distinguished between three types of multicongregation models: (1) the renting model (here, the shared-space posture), (2) the celebration model (structurally, a shared-space posture, but with more togetherness), and (3) the integrative model (perhaps closest to the language-group posture, where there is high oneness and high togetherness). See Ortiz, *One New People*, 66–72.

to fellowship with *others*."[4] He says that these are "de facto parallel congregations that are autonomous but interdependent and structurally *integrated*."[5] It is hard to discern the leadership structure of congregations that are "de facto parallel," "autonomous," "interdependent," and "structurally integrated."[6] To mitigate this confusion, our Cross-Cultural Posture Assessment Tool enables leaders to measure the degree of multiculturality, oneness, and togetherness to determine whether their church has a shared-space posture, a language-group posture, or one of the other postures.

The language-group posture typically has one senior pastor or pastoral team and an explicit vision of multiculturalism. A prime example of a church with a language-group posture is Wheaton Bible Church in West Chicago, Illinois. This church holds five services on any given Sunday: two traditional, two contemporary, and one Spanish-language service (Iglesia del Pueblo). With approximately 30 percent of the congregation being ethnically Latino, the church is intentional about maintaining a separate service to serve the Spanish-speaking community. Despite this, the church operates under one unified vision, budget, and elder board. Additionally, the church has one music band that consists of people from both the Spanish-speaking service and the English-speaking service. This intentional act of having one praise team is meant to uphold the value of being one church family that speaks different languages.

As first-generation immigrant churches reach a critical mass of English-speaking youth, they often adopt a language-group posture. While there are different models of the immigrant church,[7] these churches are often made up of one ethnicity, but they hold separate services in different languages. They conduct their main services in their language of national heritage, but their children (who typically have integrated into mainstream American culture) are often more comfortable worshiping and studying the Bible in English. Consequently, "English congregations," or services in English, are common in immigrant churches.

4. Choi, "Multicultural Church," 22–23 (emphasis original).
5. Choi, "Multicultural Church," 23 (emphasis original).
6. Choi, "Multicultural Church," 23.
7. Hong, "Intergenerational Church Conflict."

The language-group posture relies heavily on the notion that a single leadership team—with pastors from different linguistic and cultural backgrounds—can be so aligned in vision and discipleship approaches that their oneness spills over into the various congregations. Jonathan Downie is suspicious about the feasibility of such oneness without togetherness. "It is undeniable that when we create different services in different languages, we build up as many barriers as we tear down. We tell our congregants and the world around that it is okay to see languages as badges of separation. . . . The greatest danger of this model is precisely that it does not require any changes in our thinking, theology, or practice. Church goes on as normal and no one is ever put in a position where they have to cross cultural or language barriers."[8]

Peace Lutheran Church in Fresno, California, has tried to bridge this "badge of separation" by having high oneness, with low togetherness during the Sunday worship service but higher togetherness in children's ministries and weekly fellowships. The city of Fresno has thirty-five thousand ethnic Hmong, many of whom emigrated from Southeast Asia in the 1970s, so the second and third generation speak English, whereas their parents speak Hmong. Kou Seying describes the levels of oneness and togetherness at Peace Lutheran:

> The congregation is integrated in all areas of ministry, yet it serves the two primary language groups individually. There is a weekly service in the Hmong language and there is a weekly service in English. Hmong members hold elected offices in the leadership council and elders. Youth and children ministries are integrated. The congregation has called and hired staff who are fluent in both languages and cultures. The Lutheran Women's Missionary League is very well integrated with Hmong and Anglo ladies. Servant and community events are well attended by the diverse congregation.[9]

The language-group posture of immigrant churches seems to have a life cycle. In stage one, first-generation immigrants start a church for their minority language group. This is a monocultural/monoethnic

8. Downie, *Multilingual Church*, 44.
9. Seying, "Diversity and Unity," 196.

posture. Then their second-generation children prefer English, and the church shifts to a language-group posture. As the second- and third-generation immigrant families become the predominant members of the congregation, the church cycles back to a single-language church (English now), but one that is far more multiethnic than the immigrant church of their parents and grandparents.[10] Thus, they shift to the multiethnic posture.

Another model of the language group can be found among Chinese churches. What is interesting about many Chinese churches is that they often function as three distinct congregations within one church—typically, a Mandarin-speaking congregation, a Cantonese-speaking congregation, and an English-speaking congregation. Similar to the other church models mentioned above, members from all three congregations serve in the children's ministry, even though the children's Sunday school is conducted primarily in English—and the children likely will grow up to join the English-speaking congregation.

The language-group posture provides a "haven" for immigrants.[11] Note that this is similar to, but distinct from, Martí's emphasis on "havens."[12] The multiethnic church is a haven because people of various ethnicities feel at home when they are represented in the congregation or onstage, even if the worship service reflects only a single culture. In contrast, the language-group posture is a "haven" because it is a space where people can sing, pray, and study the Bible in the language and style they know best.

Andrea is the child of immigrants from South America who pastored a Spanish-speaking church in Southern California. She served in their church as a worship leader and youth leader. Now that she is raising a family, she and her husband want their children to be part of a church that has both Spanish and English ministries: "We knew specifically we wanted help with the fundamentals of raising a teenage boy, and also our daughter; and the Hispanic church that we attended just didn't really have anything for that, and we knew the

10. Mullins, "Life-Cycle of Ethnic Churches."
11. Choi, "Multicultural Church," 37.
12. Martí, "Mosaic on Mission."

Anglo churches were the ones that had all the amazing kids' programs and youth camps. So we wanted to expose our kids to living a life of faith that wasn't boring and just provide them the tools necessary in what is their language."

Later, Andrea elaborated on the difficulty she found in trying to raise her English-speaking children in a Hispanic church:

> It was mainly a childcare type of thing. Most of the churches that my parents had led, the curriculum was the most affordable option, which didn't always include the best—but that's what the churches could do. And a lot of the people that were willing to teach the classes were not fully fluent in English, so that was kind of a struggle, even with our kids. They would just have a hard time connecting, and it was just a disconnect from the teacher to all the students. Room space was also something that just didn't create the right environment for kids.

However, Andrea also wants to continue her involvement in a Hispanic church. She joined a church with a language-group posture because it helps her connect to her country of heritage:

> My heart has always been for the Hispanic, Latin community. . . . I know what it feels like to bridge your heritage, upbringing, values, but also live in the United States, where things are very different than our parents' countries. . . . This church was kind of like my pull and tug to connect back with our Spanish church. . . . Now first- and second-generation kids want to help those churches, and God has put that on their heart to just give back and modernize some things.

Darrell and Annie attend Iglesia del Pueblo of Wheaton Bible Church. Just like Andrea, Darrell and Annie longed to worship God in their heart language. Darrell shared, "I grew up speaking Spanish. So part of the reason I attend the Spanish service is I just need to feed my soul. I can sing in Spanish. I can hear a sermon in Spanish. I can talk to other believers in Spanish. And it's just a different feel than an Anglo church. . . . I enjoy the English church and it can speak to my heart, but I mean, I'll find myself maybe moved to tears singing a song in Spanish." Additionally, Darrell explained that because extended families are very important in

Latin American culture, the church becomes a new version of the extended family.

For Annie, the fact that people in the English service did not reciprocate the closeness really hurt her:

> In Latin American culture, we are very physical people, we like to hug. So if I see someone once and we have one small conversation, and I see them again tomorrow, I'll treat them like my best friend, like I would hug you. And so the first shock for me was something like that. I saw a friend from the English service, and she saw me and I saw her. And she saw me seeing her, and she didn't say hi. She acted like she had never seen me before, and I was heartbroken. From that moment, I started having a very deep and difficult process. I was talking to my husband and he was like, "It's not personal. She's not the only one. The culture, the way they interact is like that. So what can you do?"

Furthermore, Annie also noted the fact that she tried attending the English service but had a difficult time connecting. "I started going to the English service, but I couldn't find myself. I was like, 'I don't understand what they're talking about. I must not speak English because these people are talking and talking and I can't even get one word in.'"

During our church visits, we noticed that Anglo Americans also attended services in other languages. For instance, Kathy, an Anglo member of a church with a language-group posture, attends the Chinese service. She knew that she wanted to be surrounded by a multiethnic community because she remembered having learned so much from cultural others when she was in a Bible study during her college years: "In college I had this cool experience just studying the Bible with people from very different backgrounds. I was in England and I just felt like there is so much that you can learn about the Bible from people who are different from you because of the cultural background and how they see the Bible. I got so excited about that. And so my whole life, that's been a thread of thinking that I would love to get to know other Christians who understand the Bible in such a different way."

This heterophily birthed within her the desire to continue attending a multiethnic church even after she moved back to the United States. During interviews, Kathy and her husband Ethan (also an Anglo), not only mentioned the benefit of hearing from multiple perspectives when studying Scripture but also highlighted the blessing of close relationships and friendships they formed with people of other ethnicities at their church. They shared that when they first visited their current church after they had moved to the Midwest, they immediately felt welcomed: "None of the other churches were nearly as friendly, we just really felt welcomed, and we continued to go. . . . When we had our child, they had a meal train, and they helped out a lot. And we just have a lot of good friends. And it seems like going to an all-White church would be weird now."

The Difficulties of the Language-Group Posture

Togetherness and lack of togetherness both pose difficulties for congregations that speak more than one language. The pastoral team of Mosaic Church of Central Arkansas shared that they had experimented with various strategies to better serve their multiethnic congregation. These included providing headsets for translation and offering simultaneous interpretation during the service. However, they found that headsets unintentionally created a sense of hierarchy, reinforcing the perception that English was the primary language. And consecutive translation, while more inclusive, often caused services to run long and feel disjointed.

As the Spanish-speaking congregation grew, the senior pastor of Mosaic Church, Harry Li, shared a pivotal moment: The English-speaking service chose to move into the church's unfinished warehouse space so the Spanish service could use the main sanctuary. This deliberate choice was made to honor and uplift the Spanish-speaking members, making them feel valued and central to the life of the church. Pastor Harry further noted that while Mosaic Church prefers to form discipleship groups around heart language, the leadership is intentionally and strategically working to bridge language barriers.

Additionally, while the language-group posture can ensure a level of comprehension and connection, not all members of a language community share the same culture. Spanish speakers from South America have dialects, foods, and traditions different from those of Spanish speakers from Mexico. Three Spanish-speaking participants from South America mentioned (perhaps with hyperbole) that they didn't understand Mexican Spanish, and explained that South Americans do not identify tacos as their food of heritage. One participant from Mexico mentioned feeling visible now that the church has incorporated mariachi music and piñatas, but they noted that these are endemic to Mexican culture, not the rest of Latin America.

Low togetherness also hinders cohesion. An English speaker who is active at a church that has a Spanish fellowship was fairly unfamiliar with the Spanish congregation. "I feel like it's pretty separate, like they're doing their own thing. And really the only time I've seen much crossover is when there's an all-church prayer night, where they do incorporate the Spanish ministry—especially some of the worship leaders—into the songs."

Similarly, a pastor who currently serves at a church that hosts three separate language services stated, "It's just not realistic. There has to be an acceptance that we're three churches. But when you start talking that way, the other congregations get really angry, defensive. They talk about unity, but they don't know how to achieve it."

Enrico, a member of a predominantly English-speaking church with a Spanish fellowship, confessed, "Well, it is always said that we are one church, but in the end we are a ministry. Because it is also said that it is a ministry. So we are not a 'church' church. . . . We don't have much voice in many things. I mean, yes, they say it is one church in theory. Well, in my opinion, we are less like a 'church' church."

Then Enrico reflected on the progress that has been made in togetherness, causing his family to feel more included: "The needs of those of us who are here are heard more. We are making ourselves heard more, better known, and more taken into account. The Spanish ministry is getting more recognition. So as we are growing, they are giving us more. I feel like we are more part of the predominantly English-speaking church now."

It was clear in interviewing people who attended churches with a language-group posture, when they referred to their church, many were not thinking about the larger church context but rather the language service that they attended. For instance, Darrell, who attends Iglesia del Pueblo, the Spanish-language service at Wheaton Bible Church in West Chicago, said, "The only reason I go there is for Iglesia del Pueblo. I don't have any kind of emotional connection to the larger church, and I don't really care."

Acts 15:1–32: A Biblical Example of the Language-Group Posture

The language-group posture reflects the concessions made to the gentile church in Acts 15:1–32. Here, some Jewish Christians were teaching gentiles that in order to be saved they had to become Jews, which included being circumcised and following all Jewish rituals. This upset Paul and Barnabas, leading to a heated debate. When no resolution could be reached, Paul and Barnabas traveled to Jerusalem to consult with the apostles and elders on the matter. Along the way, they shared how the gentiles had been converted, which brought great joy to the believers. However, upon arriving in Jerusalem, some believers who were Pharisees also insisted, "It is necessary to circumcise them and to order them to keep the law of Moses" (Acts 15:5). After much discussion, Paul responded, "God, who knows the heart, bore witness to them, by giving them the Holy Spirit just as he did to us, and he made no distinction between us and them, having cleansed their hearts by faith. Now, therefore, why are you putting God to the test by placing a yoke on the neck of the disciples that neither our fathers nor we have been able to bear? But we believe that we will be saved through the grace of the Lord Jesus, just as they will" (Acts 15:8–11).

In this situation, we see the church composed of different ethnic groups, including Jews and gentiles. Although some Jewish Christians initially wanted the gentiles to follow their teachings and traditions, the leaders ultimately reached a consensus that the gentiles did not need to identify with the Jewish culture in order to be part of the Christian community, but the Jewish believers would maintain many of those customs (Acts 21:26). The disparate traditions were respected.

The Greek Christians would need to make some compromises as well, but they were recognized as a distinct worshiping community.

Similar to what we see in Acts 15, the language-group posture describes a church that offers opportunities for various ethnic groups to worship in their own cultural styles and languages. There is no need for one ethnic group to become like the other, as there are multiple services and various languages and cultural expressions available for people to worship.

CHAPTER SUMMARY

Churches with the language-group posture exhibit high oneness, high multiculturality, and (typically) high inclusionary vision but have low togetherness (so that various language groups can worship and study Scripture in the language they know best). And like Wheaton Chinese Alliance Church, they may even have low ethnic diversity. Offering multiple services in various languages requires a consistent vision-casting related to the "brand" of the church and a high level of coordination to ensure that the discipleship plan (sermons, small groups) is implemented across language groups. Because there is high oneness in this posture, leaders and members maintain a sense of ownership of the church, regardless of which service they attend.

Things to Watch for with the Language-Group Posture

- Ensure that the various language groups are not completely isolated as a means of avoiding the ethnic Other.
- Be aware of a spirit of competition that may develop among the various language groups.
- Take note of cultural clashes that may arise between language groups when cultural practices or values are different.

A Sunday at The Grove Community Church

I (Ken) drive on campus at 11:00 a.m. and think to myself, "I may have seen other churches with a soccer and baseball field, but this is the only church I've ever seen with a pickleball complex." It is also the only church I've seen with cottages on site expressly built as temporary housing for the homeless.

I am directed to a parking spot and notice three concrete buildings that, from the outside, look like newly built warehouses. I enter the building along with a thousand other people. Those from the Spanish and English congregations drop off their children at the same English-speaking children's ministry program.

As I walk past a gymnasium-sized room that has a sign that says "Youth," I notice the sandwich board advertising the Spanish service. I am greeted by ushers in Spanish, and they give me a bulletin that is branded exactly as the English one, including the "response card." It has upcoming events pertinent to the Spanish congregation and links to the Spanish social media pages for the church. The link for giving financially to the church is the same as the one for the English congregation. One upcoming event is a membership class. Though the membership process is the same for the Spanish and English congregations, this particular class is specifically in Spanish.

I find a seat and notice that most people know someone else in the room and are chatting quietly as the sound system plays current Latin American praise music by Marco Barrientos, Christine D'Clario, and Miel San Marcos. With a handful of exceptions (including me), the worship leaders and everyone else in the room seem to be of Latin American descent.

As the English service starts, at exactly 11:15 a.m. in the main sanctuary, the Spanish praise band promptly begins the Spanish service as well. By the time the first song starts, nearly all of the 240 seats are filled. The pastor welcomes people to The Grove and introduces himself as "Fabian, a member of the leadership team at The Grove Church." I am struck by how important this is: He was welcoming people not to the Spanish service, but to The Grove. Spanish is normalized at The Grove, and he is signaling that they are as much a part of The Grove as anyone else on campus.

The worship program follows the same formula as the English service: announcements, three praise songs, a sermon on the same topic as in the English service (today it was "Preparing for a New Year"), and then a final song. I note that on this day all four praise songs are translations of contemporary songs originally written in English by worship leaders at Bethel Music, Maverick City Music, and Elevation Worship. The translations are high quality, and each of these songs has been recorded on Spanish record labels. I wonder about the use of English worship that has been translated, because there are so many excellent Spanish praise songs originally written in Spanish, sometimes with a Latin style.

The music is not quite as "produced" as it is in the main sanctuary, but there is tremendous talent onstage for a congregation of around four hundred. Worshipers are slightly more expressive than those in the English service, though it does not feel like a charismatic service.

The pastor preaches a three-point topical sermon. Today it was on forgiveness in Acts 7. He provides pictures of a missionary family that was martyred. At times, he pauses to wait for some verbal affirmation from the congregation and, at one point, for congregants to recite the rest of a Bible verse. By the end of the sermon, he passionately pleads with the congregation to forgive their enemies.

At nearly the same moment that the English service ends in the sanctuary, the worship leaders in The Grove Español close with the last song. The pastor gives a brief benediction and tells us we are dismissed. I walk past the popup bookstore in the lobby and note that most of the books are in English, but there are some translations into Spanish as well as some books in Spanish by Latin American authors.

Why the Language-Group Posture Makes Sense for The Grove

Why not have the Spanish and English speakers worship together? Pastor Fabian explained that while English speakers may be comfortable with singing worship choruses in English and Spanish, newly arrived immigrants from Latin America do not necessarily feel comfortable in a bilingual service. "They are often poorer and feel 'less than' for not knowing English."

But this hesitancy to join the English service does not keep the Spanish constituency from desiring the highly produced worship experience that is happening in the sanctuary. "Any bilingual speaker would choose to go to the English service," because the production quality there supersedes what the smaller Spanish congregation can do in the gym. Fabian needs to provide a similar experience for the Spanish speakers. He has a specific vision in The Grove Español: "To provide the best Spanish language worship experience around."

For him, the "best experience" involves being biblically rooted, but it also involves the production quality of the worship service. Unfortunately, offering such a high level of production (and increasing the attendance as they have been) likely means not only having separate worship services but also meeting in the sanctuary at a different time, thus further decreasing togetherness. True, there are tremendous benefits to having the Spanish and English speakers come on campus at the same time (including shared experience in children's programs and at the café). But as long as the Spanish congregation uses the youth room, they are not privy to the high-quality cameras, streaming, lights, LED screens, and sound system found in the sanctuary. The gains of production quality in the main sanctuary may outweigh whatever is lost by moving the Spanish service to a time slot when the English speakers are not around. But the cost will be significant: Many people come to The Grove Español for the English-speaking children's program, and if the services are at separate time slots, they will lose that structure. For example, Emilio, who is fluent only in Spanish, explained that while he has had many positive experiences in Spanish-speaking churches, he wants "a good future for my daughter, and I saw it is a church that has many things for her. Many projects for her. So that has always been what I wanted, the best for her. So it was the better option. And I say sometimes my wife goes to the English events because she speaks more English, and I stay in Spanish. But we serve 100 percent in the Spanish ministry."

Additionally, Pastor Fabian was ambivalent about the high level of oneness when it comes to finances at his church. "When the finances are one, the English speakers control the budget. When finances are separate, the Spanish congregation gains some control over how the money is spent."

To mitigate some of these concerns, Pastor Fabian has been educating the predominantly English-speaking staff on how to be "one church with two languages." For example, they produced stickers to advertise an event. He asked, "Do we also have the stickers in Spanish?" This time they hadn't, so he printed a Spanish version fairly quickly, but the next time the staff will keep this in mind.

For The Grove, high oneness with low togetherness is intentional. Lead pastor Daniel believes that the language-group posture is the answer to the question "What is the best long-term strategy for discipleship?" Low togetherness, despite its drawbacks, allows Pastor Fabian and his team to shape pastoral care, leadership, discipleship, and worship in a way that best speaks to the Spanish-speaking members.

A Sunday at Wheaton Bible Church

Driving toward Wheaton Bible Church, I (Eunice) could see the massive compound and building while I was still about half a mile away. The church has a playground, toddlers' playroom, and even a separate café area. There are five different services every Sunday: four in English—two contemporary and two traditional—and one in Spanish, Iglesia del Pueblo. There was an extremely large foyer with a huge sign, "Bienvenidos Welcome," that greeted me. People were intermingling between services. Those who attended the earlier services had just finished, and those arriving for the Spanish service were just getting there. Everyone was stopping for coffee and fellowship, and while I waited for the service to begin, I could hear various conversations in both English and Spanish (and sometimes even in Spanglish). I noticed that all signs in the foyer (Bible verses, church information, etc.) are in both Spanish and English.

Worship began promptly at 12:15 p.m. for Iglesia del Pueblo. The worship songs were contemporary Bethel-type worship songs translated into Spanish. The congregation and the praise team both were mixes of Anglos and Latinos. The order of service was nearly identical to the English-speaking service (I had attended the English-speaking service a few weeks earlier): worship songs, dismissal of children to Sunday school, announcements, a prayer for the message, and so forth. What was interesting was that the senior pastor gave the message! Hanibal Rodriguez, the senior pastor, is Latino and speaks both English and Spanish fluently, so he often delivers the sermon to both the English-speaking service and the Spanish-speaking service. He talked about the importance of being a multicultural church because that was part of his background.

Interestingly, even though I am Korean American, I never felt out of place during the entire time in the Spanish-speaking service.

Why the Language-Group Posture Makes Sense for Wheaton Bible Church

It is a tremendous asset that the senior pastor of the church is of Latin descent and speaks both English and Spanish fluently. Obviously, if the senior pastor leads both congregations, it makes sense for there to be oneness in the preaching and discipleship plan. Imagine having to come up with two different sermons each week!

Note that in contrast to the "one name, one brand" approach at The Grove, Wheaton Bible Church uses a separate name, Iglesia del Pueblo, to refer to the "Spanish church." But having their own name has allowed those members to have more ownership of the church. They feel that Wheaton Bible Church is as much "their church" as those in the English-speaking congregation feel about it.

Interviews revealed that the leaders of the church initially had thought through the logistics of having one large service with translation. They concluded that such an approach would mean that the time allotted for everything from the sermon to announcements would have to be cut in half because everything would have to be simultaneously translated.

A separate Spanish service makes sense for this context because, as Pastor Sergio stated, the previous "English services were not attracting minorities or Latinos." Members of Iglesia del Pueblo come from as far as forty-five minutes away, so they cannot participate in the weekday programs that often draw the people of the English congregation who live nearby. As a result, it makes sense that they have separate events and programs. But there is one elder board that reflects the diversity of the church.

A Sunday at Wheaton Chinese Alliance Church

Wheaton Chinese Alliance Church hosts three services in three different languages every Sunday—English, Cantonese, and Mandarin. Interestingly, this church began as an English-speaking church around fifty years ago. Although the church is mostly monoethnic (Chinese) and does not quite meet Emerson's "80 percent rule," the English-speaking congregation has some ethnic diversity. For example, the praise team includes members from South Korea and Africa, and individuals leading prayer and announcements include Anglo Americans.

I (Eunice) attended the English service at 9:15 a.m., which was conducted entirely in English, though the pastor occasionally included a few words in Mandarin. Notably, while there is no language translation offered during the English or Cantonese services, the Mandarin service provides simultaneous English translation via headsets.

The children's Sunday school ministry is shared across congregations and is currently led by volunteers primarily from the Cantonese- and Mandarin-speaking congregations. The volunteers communicate with the children in English, even though English may not be their first language. Many youth eventually worship in the English-speaking services, and there doesn't appear to be a sense of "us versus them" among church members. However, some non-Chinese attendees noted that they tend to view only the English-speaking congregation as their church home rather than seeing all three congregations as one unified church.

Currently, the church does not have a pastor over all the congregations. Instead, each congregation is led by its own pastor. While there are occasional joint events—such as holiday services or a monthly potluck—most ministries and outreach efforts are conducted separately. Interestingly, although the potlucks are intended to foster fellowship across the congregations, members shared that people typically sit with others from their own language group, and little blending occurs.

Why the Language-Group Posture Makes Sense for Wheaton Chinese Alliance Church

Because Wheaton Chinese Alliance Church is one church with three different language services, there is one name, one budget, and one brand. Thus it has a language-group posture. What's interesting about the Chinese church is that, although it is made up predominantly of one ethnic group, it is still very multicultural and multilingual. While there are some shared cultural traditions, it makes perfect sense for the church to offer services in three different languages, reflecting the diverse languages and dialects spoken within the Chinese immigrant community.

▪ REFLECTION QUESTIONS ▪

1. How does the language-group posture reflect the biblical idea of hospitality?
2. How does the language-group posture further separate believers? How does it unite them?
3. What changes would your church need to make to move from the shared-space posture to the language-group posture?

CHAPTER 11

The Reconciling Posture

Characteristics of a Reconciling Posture

Ephesians 2:11–22

Strengths:
Cohesion across racial groups; puts biblical advocacy into action

Weaknesses:
Can be politicized; polarizing

Context:
Region that has experienced interracial tensions

Calling:
Advocacy for the marginalized

Constituency:
Multiethnic congregation

Kenneth Nehrbass

Chapter Goals

By the end of this chapter, you should be able to do the following:

- identify how churches have actively created cohesive relationships across ethnic groups
- describe ways your own church may increase its efforts in ethnic reconciliation
- explain why some churches avoid issues of reconciliation

The reconciling posture is characterized by a church that has high inclusionary vision and high ethnic diversity among the staff and within the congregation. Such a church, as Latasha Morrison says, seeks not only diversity but racial reconciliation.[1] Jemar Tisby observes, "Although activists have achieved a remarkable amount of racial progress at great cost, racism continues to plague the church. One of the reasons churches can't shake the shackles of segregation is that few have undertaken the regimen of aggressive treatment the malady requires. It seems like most Christians in America don't know how bad racism really is, so they don't respond with the necessary urgency. Even when Christians realize the need for change, they often shrink back from the sacrifices that transformation entails."[2]

In contrast to Tisby's observation about "most Christians in America," churches with a reconciling posture respond to racial issues with urgency. However, this posture does not necessarily mean that the church incorporates multiple cultural styles or languages in worship or decision-making. Although the congregation includes people from various ethnicities, they have largely assimilated into the majority culture.

Derwin Gray, founder and lead pastor of Transformation Church in Indian Land, South Carolina, implores us, "Pastor, church planter, elder and Christ-follower, you have been entrusted with the ministry of reconciliation! This calling is not optional. This calling is not debatable."[3] All churches are called to the ministry of reconciliation

1. Morrison, *Brown Faces, White Spaces*, 199.
2. Tisby, *The Color of Compromise*, 15.
3. Gray, *Building a Multiethnic Church*, 14.

(2 Cor. 5:18–20) even if they do not have a reconciling posture. Brenda Salter McNeil also states in *Roadmap to Reconciliation*, "This vision won't be fully realized until Jesus Christ returns, but in the meantime, we have been invited by God to create reconciled communities that become microcosms of the Kingdom on earth. Our ongoing collective participation in the process of reconciliation can transform our society into a place where shalom becomes a greater reality and all people can thrive."[4]

The ministry of reconciliation, however, cannot be achieved without engaging in difficult conversations. As Morrison states, "Avoiding hard conversations doesn't lead to equality or unity in Christ."[5] Angel Cartagena also notes that one of the reasons why "multiethnic churches have failed to address the issue of racism and racial injustice is that these churches are often unwilling to have open and candid discussions about race."[6] "Injuries to the church body, as Jesus teaches, are so important that one should interrupt worship to go address the problem [Matt. 5:23–24]. Much of the American church has not yet considered racism to be a serious enough sin to interrupt their regularly scheduled worship, at least not much beyond conversations and symbolic features, to repair the relationship."[7]

Fellowship Church, a church with a reconciling posture in Monrovia, California, has such conversations. On Sunday, February 23, 2025, Pastor Albert Tate wore a shirt representing his African heritage as he preached—notably, not from a pulpit, since his church is arranged in a circle. During Black History Month, he took the opportunity before preaching on 1 Corinthians 2 to address the importance of "rejecting this lie that we're supposed to be colorblind," explaining that the goal is not to avoid seeing race or cultural identity. Instead, he said, "The goal in the kingdom is to see all of that." We should see "diversity as a value" and "sit in each other's stories." He added that this is not just about singing "songs together, but hav[ing] an appreciation for our contribution in society. . . . You can be a White person and get your PhD and never understand Black culture. . . .

4. McNeil, *Roadmap to Reconciliation*, 124.
5. Morrison, *Brown Faces, White Spaces*, 197.
6. Cartagena, *Race and the American Church*, 54.
7. Tisby, *The Color of Compromise*, 199.

I can't get my GED without having to understand how to navigate White culture."

While visiting Transformation Church, I (Eunice) had the privilege of sitting down with Kylie, Nellie, and Enoch. Nellie and Enoch Johnson are Anglo Americans, and Kylie is a Latin American. Nellie and Enoch first shared that they grew up in "suburban White America," and it wasn't until they started attending Transformation Church that they realized that they were unaware of the various conversations around ethnic diversity. Enoch shared, "When I was in elementary school, living in the suburbs, the city was busing to the inner city. White kids in, busing out Black kids to the suburban schools in an effort to force diversity. . . . A lot of ignorance in an uber-White culture. . . . It was just things like that I reflect on. I didn't realize it, but I think that's part of the story for me. I had to unlearn a lot of things, culturally, theologically. I've learned how ignorant I really was as a White man in America."

Kylie grew up in a different neighborhood but moved to South Carolina just a few years ago. When she first moved into the neighborhood, she recalled having a neighbor who proudly displayed a Confederate flag in their front yard. Nellie and Enoch continued to share:

> One of the taglines we've had here [at Transformation Church (TC)] for years is that proximity breeds intimacy. And I've added to that: intimacy breeds compassion. . . . Because of that proximity of relationship, we even knew how hard it would be for [Kylie's family] to live next to someone with a Confederate flag. . . . Prior to TC, prior to having these relationships [with ethnic Others] and having these conversations and to hear the fears, we would have just been like, "Well, you know, it's a Civil War thing." Whereas now we understand the reality of what it is to live next to something like that, the reality of not being sure if you want your kids to play out in the front yard because "what are they going to overhear" or "what are they going to be subjected to?" So it's a total paradigm shift.

In the same way, Nellie and Enoch had the opportunity to build meaningful relationships with those who are of a different culture and ethnicity. Kylie also shared that she had the opportunity to build relationships with White Americans at the church:

> Growing up in a different state, I didn't have a lot of White friends. The only thing I knew about White people was stuff I saw on TV, and then even when we moved to the South and having some not great experiences with White people, I knew that in my heart I had a lot of weariness. I just had weariness around a White majority basis and I'm grateful, even as Pastor has said multiple times in public, "White people are not the enemy." . . . If you're in an antiracism space, it almost becomes like "people of color have to stick together and White people are the enemy." And I've been able to say, "No, I have great relationships and I've had great experiences with lots of people from different ethnicities. Your ethnicity, your skin color doesn't make you good or bad." We all need Jesus, and when we submit to Jesus and we take the unity that has been given to us seriously, we're able to grow together as we grow toward Christ.

Another member of Transformation Church, Rachel, shared a reflective story about her experience with racial prejudice. In her youth, she was surrounded by people of diverse cultural and religious backgrounds. And while she was comfortable exchanging pleasantries with those from different ethnicities, things changed when her daughter began dating someone with a different ethnic background. Rachel found it difficult to accept the relationship, revealing that her true feelings about the ethnic Other hadn't been fully confronted. She shared,

> My daughter wanted to date a boy, and the boy was Korean. And that's when I realized that even though I belong to the multiethnic church, it didn't hit me until it became personal to me. So that really became a huge challenge because I imagined my daughter would marry someone from our culture and it would be easy. And then I went to counseling and I heard from Pastor Derwin, and it really hit me that I'm not able to see other ethnicities as God's people. Every time when I would hear, "At the foot of the cross, everyone is equal," I didn't see that boy as another person whom Jesus died for. But getting to know that boy and seeing his beliefs in Christ—God changed my perspective altogether. Yesterday I was able to sit with him. I invited him to our home, and I was able to sit with him and have a meal with him.

The beauty of attending a church with a reconciling posture is that it not only compelled Rachel to confront her own biases and fears but also moved her to actively live out her beliefs about those from different cultural backgrounds.

The Difficulties of the Reconciling Posture

Addressing issues of difference, race, and immigration can be challenging. Curtiss Paul DeYoung and his coauthors ran into numerous cases where White members of multiracial churches believed that highlighting ethnic or racial differences was "divisive," "unimportant," or "ungodly."[8] For example, Jamaal Williams, Jarvis Williams, and Timothy Paul Jones—teaching pastors at Sojourn Church Midtown in Louisville, Kentucky—courageously broached the subject of racial disharmony in a sermon series.[9] In the second sermon in the series, Pastor Jamaal shared a story about how he was harassed by police officers while traveling with his pregnant wife, who is White. One officer even asked her if she was being held against her will. Despite Pastor Jamaal's respectful portrayal of law enforcement in the sermon series, "angry emails flooded the church's inbox. Some came from retired police officers."[10]

It seems ironic that it is impossible to address issues of racial unity without causing division. Pastor Derwin of Transformation Church told us during an interview, "Our church would probably be four times the size it is now if I chose not to disciple our people through these issues [of racial reconciliation]." Bishop Karen Oliveto described the tension caused by raising these issues at Glide Memorial United Methodist Church in San Francisco. The church "participated in rallies, held forums, and engaged in actions to highlight the gross injustices experienced by members of the black community—particularly young black men—at the hands of the police. However, within our community are also police officers, good women and men who are as outraged by their colleagues' actions as the rest of the community is. Yet they often feel attacked and vulnerable when images of the #BlackLivesMatter movement are shown."[11]

8. DeYoung et al., *United by Faith*, 172.
9. Sojourn Church, "Gospel, Race, and Injustice."
10. Williams and Jones, *In Church as It Is in Heaven*, 11.
11. Oliveto, "Ministry at the Margins," 143.

We asked a pastor how his church avoids alienating half the congregation when appearing to be "progressive." He told us, "People may call us that, but we aren't teaching anything other than the Beatitudes." At first glance, this may seem like a safe—or even correct—position. However, discipleship is not just about teaching through the Bible; it's about showing people how they can apply Scripture to questions and issues in every facet of our lives.[12] "Just" teaching the Beatitudes falls short of this. Church leaders are on solid ground if they are encouraging disciples of Jesus to apply the Beatitudes (and the "whole counsel of God") to issues of racially motivated injustices.

One seasoned pastor reminisced that deliberately addressing issues of racial reconciliation was the most challenging vision he has ever attempted throughout his ministry:

> I've been through a lot of transitions in my forty-some-odd years of ministry. I went through the charismatic renewal in the Southern Baptist Church. I went through the Willow Creek movement, where we started doing dramas and everybody's wearing sweats and flip flops. And I went through the multisite thing where now I have a pastor on a screen. But this one is the bravest one I've ever seen in my life. I thought bringing drums into the auditorium was going to get you killed! Standing up and preaching this will get you killed. I mean that seriously, this, this will get you in trouble.

Despite the controversial nature of racial reconciliation, it seems that the way to mitigate the tension is *not* by avoiding these issues altogether. Nor is it to use political discourse that alienates half of the congregation. The key seems to be the inclusion of a plurality of voices. Imagine inviting members of the church who work in law enforcement to come onstage for a conversation with Black leaders about how Christianity provides a pathway for law and order that is impartial and empathetic. Or imagine having a Palestinian Christian and an Israeli Christian discuss their visions of shalom in the Levant onstage. While not quite as dramatic as that, Pastor Daniel Bishop, at The Grove Community Church in Riverside, California, explained how the leadership team educated itself on different perspectives:

12. Nehrbass, *God's Image and Global Cultures*.

> We read Damon Horton's book [*Intensional: Kingdom Ethnicity in a Divided World*] as a staff. We read *Fault Lines* by Voddie Baucham. And we hired Albert Tate's church [Fellowship Monrovia] as consultants. I think Albert Tate's church was on one side and Voddie Baucham was on the other. And I would say that Damon Horton was maybe somewhere in the middle of those, maybe more toward Albert Tate. And we recognized, as a staff, how differently we see things. And it wasn't just "Black people think this way and White people think this way." It was like, there were some people who were Black and White on Voddie Baucham's side, and there were some people who were White and of different ethnicities on the side of Fellowship Monrovia. So I think the process, even though it was hard, as people shared, we learned that we could all have a conversation. And it's not that anyone has to be right, but can we see where we're coming from? Can we listen? Can we understand and can we live in unity together? I think we accomplished this.

Ephesians 2:11–22: A Biblical Example of the Reconciling Posture

Ephesus was a diverse, cosmopolitan city, so it's likely that the church there was diverse, comprising both Jewish and gentile believers. In his letter to the church, Paul reminds them that, despite their ethnic differences, they are called to maintain unity because Jesus Christ reconciled Jews and gentiles through his blood:

> Therefore remember that at one time you Gentiles in the flesh, called "the uncircumcision" by what is called the circumcision, which is made in the flesh by hands—remember that you were at that time separated from Christ, alienated from the commonwealth of Israel and strangers to the covenants of promise, having no hope and without God in the world. But now in Christ Jesus you who once were far off have been brought near by the blood of Christ. For he himself is our peace, who has made us both one and has broken down in his flesh the dividing wall of hostility by abolishing the law of commandments expressed in ordinances, that he might create in himself one new man in place of the two, so making peace, and might reconcile us both to God in one body through the cross, thereby killing the hostility. And he came and preached peace to you who were far off and peace to those who were near. For through him we both have access in one Spirit to the Father. So then you are no longer strangers and aliens, but you are fellow citizens

> with the saints and members of the household of God, built on the foundation of the apostles and prophets, Christ Jesus himself being the cornerstone, in whom the whole structure, being joined together, grows into a holy temple in the Lord. In him you also are being built together into a dwelling place for God by the Spirit. (Eph. 2:11–22)

A church with a reconciling posture is high in ethnic diversity, embracing and welcoming people from various ethnic backgrounds. Like the church in Ephesus, which Paul had encouraged to foster unity, the reconciling posture not only reflects diversity in the congregation but also takes the issue of racial or ethnic difference seriously. It often has a dedicated ministry focused on reconciliation, addressing both racial and relational healing.

CHAPTER SUMMARY

When Jesus hung on the cross, he reconciled us not only to the Father but also to one another. As Brenda Salter McNeil states, "We have been invited by God to create reconciled communities that become microcosms of the kingdom on earth."[13] The extension of Jesus's ministry of reconciliation is the very heartbeat of a church with a reconciling posture—one where God's kingdom is experienced here on earth. As with the advocate posture, churches with a reconciling posture maintain a high inclusionary vision, but they also have achieved a high level of ethnic diversity. They are spaces where congregants intentionally fellowship, worship, serve, and grow with people from other ethnic backgrounds.

Things to Watch for with the Reconciling Posture

- Recognize that reconciliation takes time, patience, and grace.
- Ensure that voices are not silenced in an effort to "move forward."
- Make sure those who have been most affected by conflict and/or injustice are included in the reconciliation process.

13. McNeil, *Roadmap to Reconciliation*, 124.

A Sunday at Transformation Church

In the same state where the first shots of the Civil War were fired, Transformation Church in Indian Land, South Carolina, stands as a beacon of hope. I (Eunice) arrived as people from the first service were leaving the campus and was greeted by individuals wearing blue T-shirts that said "Welcome" in multiple languages. The atmosphere was filled with genuine warmth and authentic fellowship between Black Americans and White Americans, and I also noticed many interracial couples. However, the church is not necessarily "culture-blending," as there aren't multiple languages represented in the preaching and worship music. In a conversation, one staff member mentioned the church's desire to create its own culture.

The worship was "Spirit-filled," and while it was conducted in English, there were people from various ethnic and racial backgrounds (White Americans and Black Americans) onstage. The worship leader was of Latin descent. Pastor Derwin's sermon was easy to follow, despite referencing original Greek words and offering theological explanations at times. He was not afraid to address issues of injustice, mentioning topics such as systemic racism and oppression (e.g., within the GI Bill) and stating, "I'm Black, I vote! But my number one vote is for Jesus." He also highlighted God's plan in creating multiple ethnicities.

Why the Reconciling Posture Makes Sense for Transformation Church

Transformation Church excels in ethnic diversity, oneness, inclusionary vision, and togetherness. However, since there aren't multiple "cultures" or languages represented during the service in the way we define "multicultural," the church isn't considered to be "culture-blending." The church is very open to discussing issues related to racism, and both the congregation and leadership are multiethnic. People in interracial marriages and ethnically blended families also feel welcome at Transformation Church. As one staff member mentioned, the church's vision is to create a unique "third culture"—one that isn't solely categorized as either White American or Black American.

During the focus group, participants shared their desire to better understand one another's cultural backgrounds and stories. They also acknowledged that issues of racism can no longer be pushed aside, because they directly affect their brothers and sisters. Pastor Derwin speculated that the church would likely be four times bigger if he didn't address racial issues, but the church is committed to confronting difficult and controversial topics rather than avoiding them to simply grow or please everyone. Participants also confessed that the Lord was continuing to work on their hearts, and they were grateful that Transformation Church helped them navigate their feelings of ethnocentrism. There were many tears during the focus group as people reflected on how thankful they were to be part of a church that consistently keeps racial issues at the forefront while grounding everything in the gospel.

A Sunday at Mosaic Church of Grand Rapids

Mosaic Church of Grand Rapids is a church plant about to celebrate its third anniversary. They meet every Sunday in a Boys & Girls Club, where volunteers arrive early to set up and stay late to break down. Mosaic's vision statement indicates that the church "exists to be a multi-ethnic church living out Jesus' kingdom values, bringing racial equity and gospel freedom to the city of Grand Rapids."[a] From its inception, the church has been intentional about being multiethnic and addressing issues related to racial equity and justice.

The Sunday I (Eunice) visited happened to be moving day, as the Boys & Girls Club was set to undergo renovations. As a result, the church had to pack up and relocate to another Boys & Girls Club across town. It was encouraging to see so many people get involved and volunteer to help with the move.

After a praise song, the service intentionally included a segment called "Mosaic Moment," where a member of the Racial Equity Team discussed an issue related to injustice. Additionally, the message didn't shy away from heavy topics such as colonization and focused on the vision of being multiethnic.

Why the Reconciling Posture Makes Sense for Mosaic Church

Though not a numerically large church, Mosaic was founded with the intent to reconcile racial tensions. The church strategically meets at a

Boys & Girls Club in a more diverse area of the city. Pastor Noah shared that after taking a class on culture during his seminary years, he felt called to plant a multiethnic church in the city.

While the pastor is highly intentional about bridging cultural differences, interviews made it clear that the church members are equally committed to cultivating diverse friendships and putting in the hard work of reconciliation. With church-wide discussions and events centered on racial issues, the church does not shy away from addressing topics of racism and other societal injustices. Interviews revealed that many members chose to join Mosaic Church of Grand Rapids—despite the challenges of being part of a church plant—because they are drawn by the church's commitment not only to being multiethnic but also to intentionally addressing issues of reconciliation.

a. Mosaic Church Grand Rapids, "Our Vision," accessed February 7, 2026, https://mosaicgr.org.

REFLECTION QUESTIONS

1. Is your church "colorblind" or conscious of racial, ethnic, or cultural differences?
2. What draws people to a church that has a reconciling posture?
3. If your church has a multiethnic posture, what changes would need to be made to move toward a reconciling posture?

CHAPTER 12

The Culture-Blending Posture

Characteristics of a Culture-Blending Posture

Revelation 7:9–17

Multiculturality	High
Oneness	High
Togetherness	High
Inclusionary Vision	High
Ethnic Diversity	High

Strengths:
Structure for immigrant congregations; highly relational

Weaknesses:
Scalability; attention span during simultranslation

Context:
Small congregations of recent immigrants

Calling:
Hospitality toward all cultures; disciple people in their own language

Constituency:
An established congregation with a cross-cultural heart

Kenneth Nehrbass

Chapter Goals

By the end of this chapter, you should be able to do the following:

- describe how certain churches conduct worship services that are multilingual and multicultural
- identify how the culture-blending posture may apply (or not apply) to your own church's context, call, and constituency

In a culture-blending posture, the worship experience, finances, and leadership are unified across multiple cultures, ethnicities, and language groups. The key distinction between the culture-blending posture and other postures that are high in multiculturality lies in the degree of oneness and togetherness. A culture-blending church features a single service with multiple cultural expressions—such as worship songs and/or sermons in different languages, sermons with simultaneous translation, and diverse worship styles.

First Baptist of Duluth, Georgia, is an example of a culture-blending posture. The worship service combines music of various styles, in multiple languages, and offers bulletins and translation of the services in Spanish, Korean, and Mandarin.[1] Intentionality is key here.

Wilcrest Baptist Church in Houston, Texas, now has a culture-blending posture, but earlier on, it experimented with the language-group posture: "The church planted ethnic churches on their campus. Wilcrest also experimented with alternative language services but has chosen not to continue these services in order to emphasize their unity in diversity. The polity of the church is that of a traditional, senior pastor-led, Southern Baptist congregation."[2]

In what he describes as the "beautiful community," Irwyn Ince states, "It is essential to probe our preferences . . . because we cannot ignore the fact that there is a positive aspect of in-group members. . . . So, beautiful community is the crafting of a new *we*. This is not a call for people to forget or become less aware of their ethnicity. Rather, it is a call to embrace their identity as part of a new group."[3]

1. Hearn, *Technicolor*, 101.
2. Byrd, *The Multiethnic, Multicongregational Church*, 136.
3. Ince, *The Beautiful Community*, 126.

Culture-blending worship requires the worship leaders from the various ethnolinguistic communities to all have a voice in the planning of the worship service.[4] There are *degrees* of integration, from acknowledgment (one style is dominant) to blended (a mixture) to greater degrees of collaboration in cocreating or "fusing" worship.[5]

When Quest Church in Seattle first opened its doors, Pastor Katey Hage noted that while the congregation consisted of people of various cultures and ethnicities, people still had to assimilate because the church was monocultural. It was not until the church began asking questions and really started listening to the congregation members that they realized they would have to make some serious adjustments in order to create a space where all people would feel welcomed:

> For many years we were fairly monocultural and everyone assimilated to this one particular type of [pan-Asian and White] community. But as we grew together, we kept asking questions and listening to stories and longing for a broader reach of our ethnic diversity and story and commitment to shared leadership. We had to ask questions about people's experience of the church community. So we stayed curious, we kept asking questions, and we kept paying attention when people said, "I love the idea, but I don't see myself represented in the music or the language." And we had to pay attention to those narratives, and then slowly over time, really being intentional about being open to change. So Quest has evolved in our understanding of what it means to be multiethnic. When we were addressing those cultural questions, that's when we started to realize, "Oh, we're kind of monocultural, even if we're multiethnic. What does it look like to be multicultural and to have people feel like they can come in and fully be themselves?"

We asked people who attend churches with a culture-blending posture why multiculturality with togetherness is a value to them. One participant explained that he could never go back to a "normal" (read: monocultural) church because his Anglo church felt so transactional and individualistic. At Village Church in Beaverton, Oregon, people expect to be relational: "Usually there's a warmth you feel that

4. Van Opstal, *The Next Worship*, 89.
5. Van Opstal, *The Next Worship*, 103.

you might not feel in a predominantly White church—but especially at Village, as it was when we first came not very touchy-feely, it was a more intellectual understanding of the Bible. And these other cultures have brought more relational depth to our church."

Another member explained that she has expanded her understanding of prayer due to the cross-cultural exposure at her church. Anglos "tend to pray about sicknesses," but she has noticed that often her Asian friends "pray about relationships."

As noted above, churches with a culture-blending posture integrate multiple cultures and languages in all aspects of their worship. Prior to visiting Quest Church in Seattle, I (Eunice) had the opportunity to talk with a few members about their experiences of attending a church with a culture-blending posture. Kaylee recalled visiting multiple churches when she and her husband first moved to the Pacific Northwest. She said, "On the first Sunday that we went to Quest, one of the worship songs was partially in Korean, which is for my husband, his heart language, and so he was just weeping. It was a lovely confirmation that we had found a space that would work for our family." Katie, who serves on the praise team at Quest Church, mentioned,

> The worship pastor is very intentional about making sure multiple cultures, multiple languages are represented in our worship each week, and if there is a section of a song that we're singing that is newer or that maybe we just haven't done in a while, the vocalists will talk through the pronunciation. . . . The worship pastor talks to people who are native speakers of those languages for clarification and to make sure that we are not misspelling things and not mispronouncing things to the best of our abilities, while knowing that there is certainly grace and we are doing our best to honor and do justice by the music the way it was intended to be heard.

Ashley added,

> Every week we sing in at least two languages—we know songs in Spanish, Korean, Zulu, and Swahili—which has expanded the ways in which I see the presence of God in worship. But the goal is always, even if this song or this thing isn't in your heart language, we still do

> this as a collective, knowing that for someone this expression of worship is home for them. And how do you enter in and walk alongside them? By doing that, even if it's not your preferred way, or the way you grew up, or what's familiar to you.

Now, having been a member of Quest Church for some time, Kaylee reflected not only on the beauty of experiencing multiple cultures in worship but also on the richness of being in community with people from diverse cultural backgrounds: "We were for a period of time, part of a small group, and at some point during the meeting, I realized I was the only White person in the room of a dozen people. And I thought, 'I don't actually know if I've had that experience before.' I definitely never had that experience at a church."

Katie added that the church is intentional about ensuring that multiple cultures and genders are represented in the various spaces throughout the church: "The people that are planning and inviting us to sign up will make sure that the group is not all one color and ideally not one gender in front, like when we're serving Communion or for greeting. That is also the case for the prayer team."

Another way Quest Church ensures that people of all ethnicities feel welcome is by inviting suggestions for the type of Communion bread used. As one member shared, "One of my favorite things that we do for Communion on Easter Sunday is that we take suggestions every year of what bread feels like home or tastes like home, and people come and get to pick bread. . . . One of my friends, who was Ethiopian, came the first year we had *injera*. She was like, 'Oh my gosh, I didn't expect this to impact me as much as it did, but this tastes like home.'"

As with the language-group posture (chap. 10), the culture-blending posture makes sense when immigrant communities need a place to worship in their various languages but want to build a church for their English-speaking children. Pastor Paul Park, at Free Life Community Church in Southern California, put it this way:

> I grew up in the Korean church, and they would have the Korean-speaking service, and then they would have an English ministry on the side. But the mother church would be the Korean church, where

> culturally, financially, and polity-wise, it's all run by the Korean elders. But the challenge is when you have twenty-year-olds, thirty-year-olds that don't know Korean culture as much, they don't speak the language, they're more American, and they have American jobs. And you know, their friend group is diverse. . . . And so what we do at Free Life Community Church is we still know the value of family. And so if we wanted to continue on with a separate ethnic language service, the pastor would have to know that we're not here to build the Cambodian church. We're not here to build the Vietnamese church. We're here to build the next generation. And if they understand the next generation or English-speaking diverse community, it's a good fit. I had a couple of churches that we were trying to partner with, but I don't think they understand that we're not here to build a Cambodian American service. We're here to build the next generation, which is multiethnic and multicultural.

The Difficulties of the Culture-Blending Posture

There is a "chicken and egg" dilemma with the culture-blending posture. For example, you cannot draw speakers of Hindi to your church unless your signage and songs represent Hindi, and your sermons are translated into Hindi. On the other hand, it makes little sense to start providing such translation if there is no constituency of Hindi speakers attached to the church. Another way to look at this is to say that it's not a "chicken and egg" dilemma; rather, it points to the necessity of growing the culture-blending posture organically. That doesn't mean it happens without inclusionary vision. Vision sensitizes you to the needs of speakers of other languages; it opens the possibilities for how you will meet their needs. But the "organic" aspect means that you work with speakers of other languages with whom you have a connection. As Pastor Paul Park put it, "We're not doing diversity for diversity sake; we're here to serve the community."

The culture-blending posture does not seem to be as scalable as the other six postures. How many languages can a church realistically *blend* long-term into its worship service? And how large can a church grow with this posture? In the suburbs of Portland and Seattle, Village Church and Quest Church have been able to attract several hundred multicultural enthusiasts to their special kind of church, but can they attract several thousand? One long-term lay leader said that the leadership team at Village Church was very aware of the issue of scalability when they started experimenting with the culture-blending posture: "At the time church growth experts were saying, 'That's not how you grow your church. If you do this you will ruin your church.' And Pastor Jensen [the senior pastor at that time] said, 'Well, we're going to do it anyway.' And I believe at the time he felt that this was God's calling for us." Adopting that vision has been the lifeblood of Village Church. But they did have to choose multiculturality over scalability.

Revelation 7:9–17: A Biblical Example of the Culture-Blending Posture

The culture-blending posture is the picture seen in Revelation 7: "After this I looked, and behold, a great multitude that no one could number, from every nation, from all tribes and peoples and languages, standing before the throne and before the Lamb, clothed in white robes, with palm branches in their hands, and crying out with a loud voice, 'Salvation belongs to our God who sits on the throne, and to the Lamb!'" (Rev. 7:9–10).

What we appreciate about this passage—beyond the fact that there will be a day in the not-so-distant future when all peoples will gather before the throne to worship the Lamb—is that when John saw this vision of the throne room, he recognized that there were people from different nations, tribes, and languages. In other words, the throne room is not monocultural, but multicultural; people do not lose their cultural identities. Not only this, but people speak in their own languages as they worship the Lamb. Reading this passage reminds us that the coming together of different *ethnē* to worship the Lamb is not only beautiful but also deeply worshipful. As Josh Davis and Nikki Lerner assert, "There is not a Hispanic worship time at 9:00 a.m. around the throne while a Somali worship service happens somewhere else in heaven."[6]

6. Davis and Lerner, *Worship Together*, 16.

John's vision in Revelation 7 reflects the culture-blending posture, where people from multiple cultures, ethnicities, and languages are not only present in the congregation but also represented in leadership and worship teams. Sunday services incorporate songs from a variety of ethnic cultures and languages, and sermons are delivered by people from different ethnic backgrounds.

CHAPTER SUMMARY

The culture-blending posture is one where multiple cultures, languages, and ethnicities come together in a single service. For example, prayers may be offered in Korean, announcements made in English, and the sermon delivered in Spanish. People from diverse ethnic backgrounds not only gather, bringing their whole selves, but also experience worship alongside others in their respective languages. The culture-blending posture can best be understood by envisioning John's vision of all nations, tribes, and languages gathered around the throne in Revelation 7.

Things to Watch for with the Culture-Blending Posture

- Be mindful of a boastful spirit that may look down on others who do not share the same posture.
- Maintain a posture of humility when engaging in cross-cultural relationships.
- Recognize that bridging cultures can be challenging. Pursue relationships that provide accountability and encouragement.

A Sunday at Village Church

As I (Ken) walk into the chapel of Village Church in Beaverton, Oregon, for the 8:15 a.m. service, I see wooden buttresses and stained-glass windows without images. The only image in the building, in fact, is the cross above the baptismal. A large screen displays this motto: "Befriending across boundaries, peacemaking in the world." The pews have been removed, and twenty round tables have been set up; each table has about four people at it who seem to know one another. On the one hand, I am a bit nervous about sitting at a table with strangers for a church service, but on the other hand, I realize I've shown up for a different kind of church service.

I notice a small table near where an altar would have been when the chapel was used as a sanctuary. There are three candles on it and trays for the Communion elements.

Announcements play on the large screen. They have clearly arranged for a nonnative Spanish speaker to do the announcements in Spanish, and a nonnative English speaker repeats the announcements in English. This sends a message to me that people with accents are welcome here and that members in the church try to learn one another's languages. I notice that the woman seated next to me at my table has a Korean and English version of the Bible.

The lead pastor, Dr. Paul Choi, then makes announcements, including updates on two church staff members who have had unprecedented issues in getting their work visas extended. One of these international workers who has been affected by the work visa limit is the worship leader. Today she leads the first service alone at the piano. She sings "Great Is Thy Faithfulness" and "Great Are You, Lord." I take note that the songs are displayed in English, Korean, and Spanish, but only the English lyrics are sung.

There is a responsive prayer in all three of these languages, but it is read only in English. To continue the multilingualism, the Scripture reading was done in advance on video, and the subtitles are in Chinese, Japanese, English, Spanish, and Korean, with English narration.

The pastor of intergenerational ministry preaches, and congregants know to open the church app and download the "weekend package," which contains an AI-generated translation of the sermon in Japanese, Korean, Spanish, and Mandarin.

We take the Communion elements back to the table, and Pastor Choi quietly explains to me that Communion at the table represents "communion of the saints, and communion with the saints." We then sing "Build My Life"[a] and receive a benediction with the words displayed in three languages on the screen.

Between the services, I stop by the coffee shop in the main lobby. There is a beautiful art installation, probably twenty feet wide and ten feet tall, in orange and brown hues, of the Lord's Prayer in Spanish, English, Korean, and Chinese. I note another beautiful art installation at the main entrance that lists the church's mission statement in Korean, Arabic, English, Japanese, Spanish, Chinese, and Hindi. It reads, "Compelled by the love of Jesus, we exist to love the Triune God and to love our neighbors as ourselves."

The welcome table has a brochure for immigration resources, legal help, resettlement agencies, citizenship classes, and ESL courses. Next to the welcome table, I see that tables are set up for Japanese and Spanish speakers to take a small FM device and listen to the service in translation. Pastor Choi explained to me that the church tried for a while to have the translation broadcast over Wi-Fi to people's cell phones and tablets, but despite high-speed internet, they could not supply the bandwidth and found FM to be more reliable. I peek into the small recording booths where the translators do their simultaneous translations.

At 10:30 a.m. I pass by greeters wearing name tags that have greetings in six languages. I enter the sanctuary, which seats about five hundred, and it's mostly full. There is no point in trying to tally up the "80 percent rule" to see if the church meets the criteria for a high ethnic diversity, because by the time I sit down, I have already experienced a mini–United Nations conference! In fact, it seems that the church reflects the demographics of the Portland metropolitan area.

The worship band leads us in singing "Great Things"[b] and "Way Maker."[c] As with the first service, the lyrics are in three languages, but now Pastor Choi, who also plays guitar and sings well, is able to prompt the congregation when to sing the choruses in Spanish or in Korean. Nearly twenty minutes of the service are dedicated to an update on missionaries serving in a "restricted-access nation." The update includes seven testimonies, some given in English and some in Korean with English subtitles.

The house lights come on, and the passing of the peace lasts five minutes. It becomes clear to me that since the congregation knows the passing of the peace will be this long, they will truly use the time to go around and greet acquaintances and friends.

Pastor Drew Fajen delivers the sermon, on "Let the Children" (Matt. 19:14). I see several people using their translation devices. We walk forward for Communion elements. Gluten-free elements are available in four alcoves along the sides of the building. We end the service by singing "Build My Life."

The congregation is then dismissed into "fellowships." Young adults share fellowship in one room, the Korean fellowship is in the chapel, and the Spanish fellowship is downstairs. They sit at tables and discuss the message.

Why the Culture-Blending Posture Makes Sense for Village Church

How would a church with a culture-blending posture decide which languages to broadcast on a screen, or which languages to provide simultaneous translation for? The languages represented at Village Church are those of the various ethnolinguistic "fellowships" in the church. The culture-blending posture happened organically, as various house churches (in the case of the Japanese fellowship) or small congregations that speak Korean or Spanish or Hindi sought a partnership with a well-established and hospitable church. Starting with a Korean fellowship and then expanding to other languages, Village Church has developed a cross-cultural posture that can strengthen these ethnic fellowships. While the multiethnic posture makes sense for communities with high ethnic diversity and high fluency in English, the culture-blending posture makes sense in a context with high multilingualism. Portland has many multinational corporations that employ foreign workers who are less fluent in English. In fact, at Village Church, I came across foreign workers from Nike and Intel on the Sunday I visited. There is some instability in any congregation that is made up of expatriate workers. The culture-blending posture ensures stability for these various fledgling ethnolinguistic fellowships.

Village Church can meet the needs of foreign workers and immigrants in their community, and that level of community interaction opens the door for sharing the gospel. Roy, who has been a part of Village for decades, teaches ESOL (English for Speakers of Other Languages) twice a week:

> A lot of my students come from Asia, and they're here for the first time. Some of them are newly married. They don't know anybody, and so they find a community of like-minded people even from different countries. Like, Japanese and Koreans get together. And they're all in this together. And so it's a place where they can find community. And then, of course, it gives us an opportunity to talk about our faith. So we do teach English, but we are a church, and particularly at Thanksgiving, Christmas, and Easter, we talk about those holidays and invite the students to join us for those services. And we've had a couple of recent examples of students who have become followers of Jesus through this whole process. And we're really thrilled about that.

a. Younker et al., "Build My Life."
b. Wickham and Myrin, "Great Things."
c. Sinach, "Way Maker."

A Sunday at Quest Church

I (Eunice) know someone who visited Quest Church in Seattle a few years ago. She told me that there was something distinctly different about the atmosphere. I now understand what that person meant. At Quest Church, the phrase "Everyone Belongs" isn't just a slogan. It's something they actively live out.

This welcoming spirit is evident not just in the people who attend but in every aspect of the church. The layout, the resources, and even the announcement boards all reflect an intentional posture of hospitality. For example, the sanctuary includes a children's quiet corner at the back where families can bring their little ones to read or color quietly during the service. Additionally, there are tables with various supplies for both adults and children (e.g., noise-canceling earmuffs, fidget toys, coloring pages, and crayons). A wide range of resources—from community groups to books and event information—is available to support those exploring topics like inclusivity, justice, and mental wellness. What Micah shared during an interview was quite evident both in the physical space and among the people that gathered for worship: "In practice, we're always trying to find connections despite our differences, while recognizing at the same time, I might do something this way or I might sing this song this way. We still try to find common ground or commonality, like 'How can we listen to someone else's story and share our own story?' I love that that's always been a priority at Quest and I hope it never changes."

What stood out most to me is that Quest Church intentionally creates space not only for ethnic diversity but also for those who may have felt marginalized within the broader society.

The service officially began at 10:00 a.m. I noticed that people continued to trickle in until 10:15 a.m. Both the congregation and the worship team reflect a beautiful diversity of cultures and ethnicities, and there seems to be genuine unity among them. One moment that particularly stood out to me was when an older Korean couple walked into the lobby and were warmly greeted with a respectful bow by someone of a different ethnic background. Each of the various segments during worship was led in English by people of different ethnic backgrounds, and while there was no formal translation, the praise team included a Spanish chorus in their worship. During announcements, a staff member reaffirmed Quest's ethos as a multicultural, intergenerational church.

The pastoral team includes four pastors from different ethnic backgrounds, each bringing their own cultural perspective when they preach. During an interview, Jessie mentioned that while "a lot of multicultural churches have a diversity of people, they are White culture churches. But Quest really doesn't feel that way to me. When Pastor Brenda preaches, it is Black church. When Pastor Aaron preaches, it is Korean church."

This week it was Pastor Aaron's turn to give the message. It was "Korean church." After the service, I was invited to a trauma-informed yoga class. People of various ethnicities gathered together in what became an intimate time of reflection and movement—a fitting continuation of the welcoming, healing space that Quest Church aims to be.

Why the Culture-Blending Posture Makes Sense for Quest Church

Quest Church is intentional about creating a safe, multiethnic space not only for its congregation but also within its pastoral leadership and staff. As mentioned earlier, each pastor brings their own cultural perspective—not just in preaching but in how they lead. The unique gifts and backgrounds of each individual are seen not as burdens or obstacles but as strengths to be celebrated.

During interviews, several participants shared that the church intentionally includes at least one or two songs in a different language each Sunday. Rather than offering separate services based on language, Quest Church brings everyone together to worship in a shared space. The result is a beautiful mosaic of voices, languages, and cultures worshiping side by side every week.

REFLECTION QUESTIONS

1. What would you enjoy most about attending a church with a culture-blending posture?
2. If your church tried to adopt a culture-blending posture, what would be the biggest challenge?
3. In what ways can your church welcome people from different ethnic backgrounds so that they would feel a sense of belonging?

Conclusion

It is now time to revisit this book's learning goals as outlined in the introduction. You should be able to distinguish between seven cross-cultural postures and to identify the five MOTIVEs (Multiculturality, Oneness, Togetherness, Inclusionary Vision, Ethnic Diversity) that shape those postures. At the end of this conclusion are two figures that can help to visualize these concepts. The model shown in the figure titled "Five Overlapping Values Create Seven Cross-Cultural Postures" depicts the way that churches' responses to these five overlapping MOTIVEs result in seven different cross-cultural postures (the hybrid posture cannot be depicted below). The flowchart titled "Mapping Your Church's Cross-Cultural Posture" may help you determine the cross-cultural posture of your church.

The learning goals in the book's introduction also promise that you will be able to evaluate the seven cross-cultural postures. Such a task is complex, but the table below provides some shorthand for you to think through each approach. The table shows the ethnic composition, structure, and characteristics of seven different cross-cultural postures.[1]

1. Others have tried to capture the different postures and to show the differences between each approach. In comparison to the three models in DeYoung et al., *United by Faith*, 165, the multiethnic posture here would be their *assimilated* church, the language-group posture seems close to their *pluralist* model, and the culture-blending posture is close to their *integrated* model. In comparison to Elizabeth Drury's

The Ethnic Composition, Structure, and Characteristics of Seven Different Cross-Cultural Postures

Posture	Ethnic Composition and Cohesion	Organizational Structure	Characteristics
Shared-Space Posture	Multiple ethnicities but not together	Separate leadership teams, finances, and brand	Sponsorship of nascent ethnic congregations; occasional shared worship experiences; low commitment to one another
Monocultural/ Monoethnic Posture	One ethnicity	One leadership team, finances, brand	Consistency; a single worship style and leadership style
Advocate Posture	Mostly one ethnicity	One leadership team, finances, brand	Programming related to racial reconciliation; agreement in this vision
Multiethnic Posture	Multiple ethnicities together	One leadership team, finances, brand	Single worship style; interethnic relationships; people of various ethnicities who are fluent in English and prefer majority-culture worship experiences
Language-Group Posture	Multiple cultures, languages, ethnicities, but not together	One leadership team, finances, brand	Monocultural worship experiences within each group's worship service; services in languages other than English targeting first-generation immigrants; high commitment to a shared vision of reaching the various language/cultural groups
Reconciling Posture	Multiple ethnicities together	One leadership team, finances, brand	Single worship style; intentional effort put into racial reconciliation
Culture-Blending Posture	Multiple cultures, languages, ethnicities together	One leadership team, finances, brand	Various cultures represented in a single, shared worship experience; various leadership styles; intentionality in representing and understanding other cultures

---

taxonomy in "Leading the Multiethnic Church," the shared-space posture would be considered *renters* or *investors*, the multiethnic posture would be considered *co-workers*, and the culture-blending posture (and perhaps the multiethnic posture as well) would be *siblings*. Ed Lee, founding pastor of Mosaic Community Covenant Church in Sugar Land, Texas, developed a model representing the differences between seven types of multicultural churches (see DeYmaz and Li, *Ethnic Blends*, 222), but it lacks explanation for the factors or values that explain how churches arrive at these various postures.

The Cross-Cultural Posture Assessment Tool (CPAT) demonstrates "goodness of fit" if the majority of churches fit into one of the other seven postures. Churches that do not fit any of these postures receive the label "hybrid." Thirty-one percent of participants who took the CPAT in this study rated their church as "hybrid." This indicates that the model was a "good fit" for only about 69 percent of participants. We are not certain at this point if this means that an additional posture needs to be added or if the language of the five indices must be adjusted to improve clarity and to reduce bias in participants' responses. (For example, a number of participants gave low scores across the board, indicating overall disapproval of their church. This results in a hybrid posture, but it also raises this question: How is it possible to have a church that has low oneness and low togetherness but is also monocultural? What kind of church would this be?) Perplexing responses present an opportunity for church leaders to discuss how congregants interpret the church's five MOTIVEs.

Lastly, this book promises that you will have empathy for people who find a home at each of the seven postures. There are good reasons for some churches to land on the shared-space posture, for others to choose a language-group posture, and so on. However, leaders should be sure that the posture taken by their church is intentional rather than subconscious and unguided. They may read this book and discern steps they can take to move from one posture to another.

Perhaps the reason it has been so difficult to define "multicultural church" is that there are so many different ways for churches to *be* multicultural! And the fact that there are various approaches is encouraging: Churches have different callings, constituencies, and contexts. Each of the postures has its strengths and weaknesses. A language-group posture makes sense for a church that is called to support first-generation immigrants, but it lacks the cohesiveness or togetherness found in single-site congregations. A multiethnic posture suits native English speakers of various backgrounds but may elide an emphasis on racial and cultural issues. The reconciling posture is found in contexts where multiethnic congregations grasp a vision of activism and reconciliation, but if it takes a strong political stance, it risks alienating congregants. A shared-space posture allows established or declining churches to sponsor fledgling churches without impinging on their autonomy, but it lacks oneness. The culture-blending posture is a vision of heaven, but it requires significant buy-in from the congregation, and it is hard to imagine that such a model is scalable.

Suggestions for Further Research

The CPAT developed in this study can be used in further quantitative research. For example, inferential statistics can be used to measure correlations between various cross-cultural postures and other variables:

- How does the cross-cultural posture of the church correlate with congregants' attachment to those who are from different ethnicities or cultures?
- How does the cross-cultural posture of the church correlate with the congregants' level of cultural humility?
- What is the correlation between denomination (especially the denominational theology) and cross-cultural postures?
- Are churches with a culture-blending posture more likely to be new church plants or to be established churches?
- How does the average age of the congregation members correlate with the cross-cultural posture of the church?

Additionally, because the context of this study is North American churches, further research in other cultural contexts would be beneficial to better understand the cross-cultural postures of churches globally.

Concluding Challenge

Models for a Multicultural Church presents logistic, linguistic, and social challenges. But God has called us to overcome those obstacles. "My house will be called a house of prayer for all nations" (Isa. 56:7 NIV). How is that prophecy being applied to your calling, constituency, and context?

We encourage you to go to http://www.nehrbass.info/cpat.html where the CPAT can be taken online. Have others in your church take the assessment as well. Discuss the results. Which of the five MOTIVEs can your church increase? Is there something about your church's score that suggests your church should move toward one of the other cross-cultural postures?

Five Overlapping Values Create Seven Cross-Cultural Postures

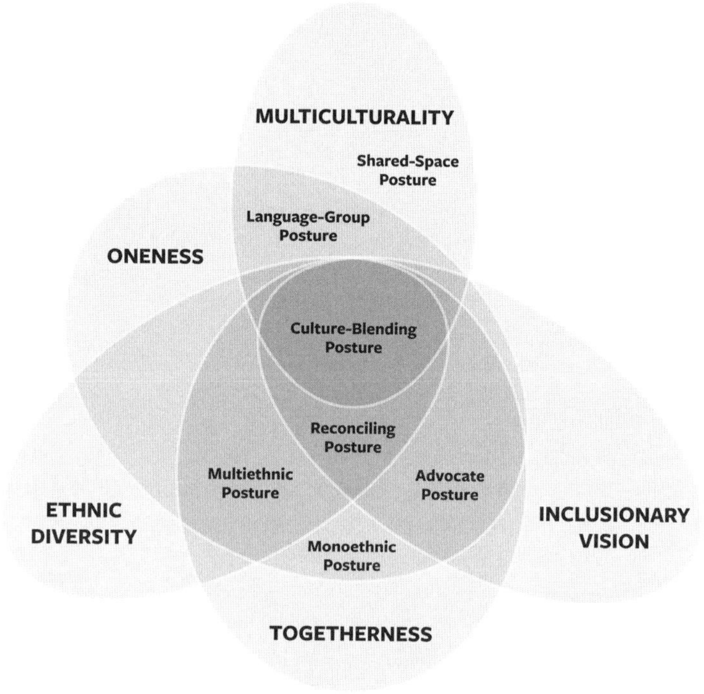

Shared-Space Posture: Multiple congregations sharing the same space; worship sevices are in multiple languages and style; separate budgets, child programming, meetings, and leadership. *Acts 2:1–41*

Language-Group Posture: Shared vision and "branding" but separate worship meetings due to different languages and styles. *Acts 15:1–32*

Culture-Blending Posture: Worship, finances, and leadership are integrated across multiple cultures, ethnicities, and languages. *Rev. 7:9–17*

Reconciling Posture: Congregation is multiethnic; church addresses issues of race; but does not have multiple cultures represented in worship/decision making. *Eph. 2:11–22*

Monoethnic Posture: Limited ethnic, cultural diversity, and limited vision for becoming diverse. *1 Pet. 2:9*

Advocate Posture: Congregation is more than 80 percent one race/ethnicity; worship is monocultural, but is committed to racial, cultural unity. *Acts 10:34–48*

Multiethnic Posture: Congregation is from multiple nations or ethnic backgrounds representing the urban shifts or diversity of the city; worship experience homogeneous; sermons may be translated; the church does not have an explicit commitment to reconciliation. *Acts 6:1–7*

Kenneth Nehrbass and Eunice Hong

Mapping Your Church's Cross-Cultural Posture

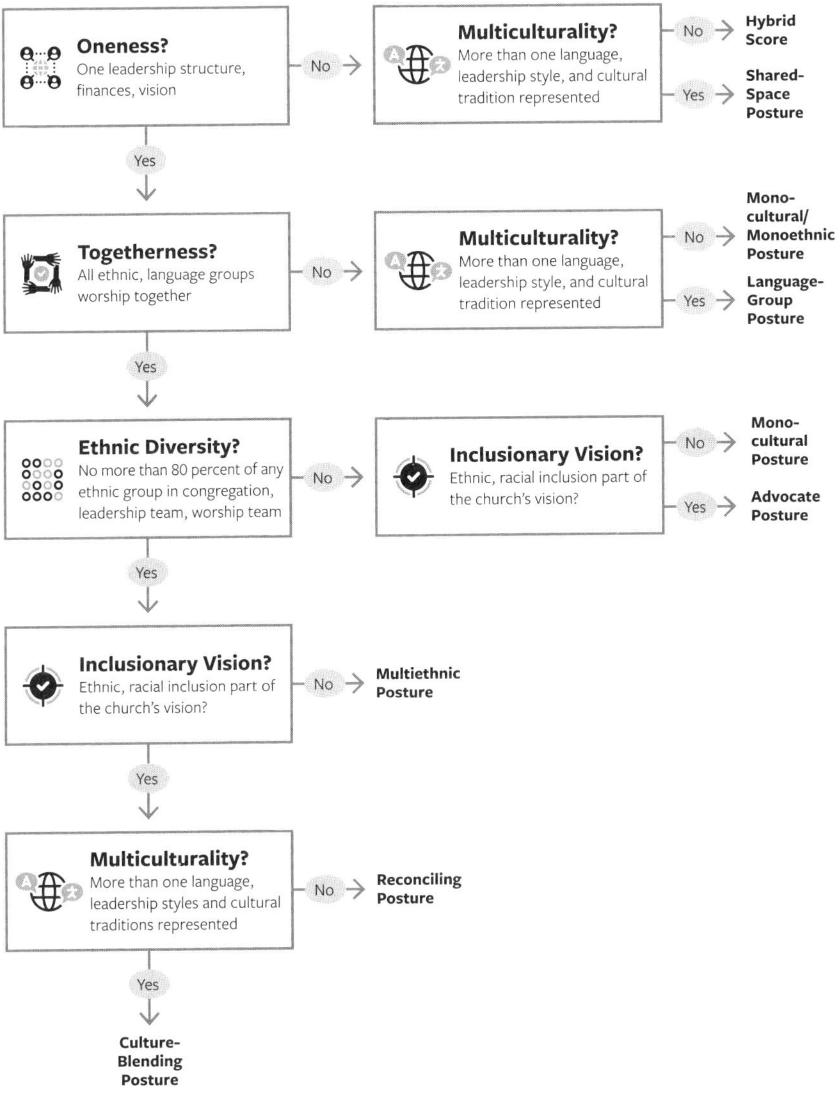

Kenneth Nehrbass and Eunice Hong

Acknowledgments

We thank the following agencies for their support in funding this research: the Internal Research Grant (IRG-2025-1125) through the Office of the Provost and the Faculty Development Committee at California Baptist University; the G. W. Aldeen Faculty Development Grant at Wheaton College; and the Vital Worship, Vital Preaching Grant at Calvin Institute of Christian Worship.

We are especially grateful to the dozens of church leaders and church members who gave us some of their time to participate in this study.

Bibliography

Anderson, David. *Gracism: The Art of Inclusion*. InterVarsity, 2023.

Anderson, David, and Margarita Cabellon, eds. *Multicultural Ministry Handbook: Connecting Creatively to a Diverse World*. InterVarsity, 2010.

Anderson, David, and Brent Zuercher. *Letters Across the Divide: Two Friends Explore Racism, Friendship, and Faith*. Baker Books, 2001.

Azumah, John, and Cheikh Anta Babou, eds. *Territoriality and Hospitality: Christian and Muslim Perspectives*. Langham Global, 2024.

Baker, Mark, ed. *Proclaiming the Scandal of the Cross: Contemporary Images of the Atonement*. Baker Academic, 2006.

Barna, George. *The Power of Vision: Discover and Apply God's Vision for Your Life and Ministry*. Gospel Light, 2009.

Barna Group. "Report Examines the State of Mainline Churches." Barna Group, December 7, 2009. https://www.barna.com/research/report-examines-the-state-of-mainline-protestant-churches/.

Barron, Jessica, and Rhys Williams. *The Urban Church Imagined: Religion, Race, and Authenticity in the City*. New York University Press, 2017.

Bowers, Laurene Beth. *Becoming a Multicultural Church*. Wipf & Stock, 2006.

Branson, Mark, and Juan F. Martínez. *Churches, Cultures and Leadership: A Practical Theology of Congregations & Ethnicities*. 2nd ed. IVP Academic, 2023.

Byrd, David. "The Multiethnic, Multicongregational Church: Developing for Urban Church Revitalization." PhD diss., Mid-America Baptist Theological Seminary, 2013.

Cannon, Mae Elise. *Social Justice Handbook: Small Steps for a Better World*. InterVarsity, 2009.

Cartagena, Angel. *Race and the American Church: A Systems Approach to Healing and Reconciliation*. Kingdom Faith Books, 2023.

Chang, Geoff. "Reflections on 'One Assembly' and the Immigrant Church." 9Marks, July 3, 2020. https://www.9marks.org/article/reflections-on-one-assembly-and-the-immigrant-church/.

Choi, Hyun. "A New Form of a Multicultural Church for Today's Multilingual Context." PhD diss., Asbury Theological Seminary, 2023.

Christerson, Brad, Korie L. Edwards, and Michael O. Emerson. *Against All Odds: The Struggle for Racial Integration in Religious Organizations*. New York University Press, 2005.

ChurchSalary. "How Multisite Churches Pay Campus Pastors." ChurchSalary, September 11, 2023. https://www.churchsalary.com/content/articles/how-multisite-churches-pay-campus-pastors.html.

Collinge, Ian. "Intercultural Worship: A Contemporary Understanding of Church and Worship in the Global Age." In *Arts Across Cultures: Reimagining the Christian Faith in Asia*, edited by Warren R. Beattie and Anne M. Y. Soh. Fortress, 2023.

Cornell, Stephen, and Douglas Hartmann. *Ethnicity and Race: Making Identities in a Changing World*. Sociology for a New Century. Pine Forge, 2006.

Davis, Josh, and Nikki Lerner. *Worship Together: In Your Church as in Heaven*. Abingdon, 2015.

D'Clario, Christine, Josh Morales, Daniel Calveti, Jacobo Ramos, Becky Collazos, and Travy Joe Pagan. "Danzando." On *Grande y Fiel (En vivo)*. Gateway Worship Español, 2022.

DeYmaz, Mark. *Building a Healthy Multi-Ethnic Church: Mandate, Commitments, and Practices of a Diverse Congregation*. Jossey-Bass, 2020.

DeYmaz, Mark, and Harry Li. *Ethnic Blends: Mixing Diversity into Your Local Church*. Zondervan, 2010.

DeYmaz, Mark, and Harry Li. *Leading a Healthy Multi-Ethnic Church: Seven Common Challenges and How to Overcome Them*. Zondervan, 2010.

DeYoung, Curtiss Paul, Michael O. Emerson, George Yancey, and Karen Chai Kim. *United by Faith: The Multiracial Congregation as an Answer to Race*. Oxford University Press, 2003.

Dieppe, Tim. "What's Wrong with Multiculturalism?" Christian Concern, February 27, 2018. https://christianconcern.com/resource/whats-wrong-with-multiculturalism/.

Dougherty, Kevin D., Mark Chaves, and Michael O. Emerson. "Racial Diversity in U.S. Congregations, 1998–2019." *Journal for the Scientific Study of Religion* 59, no. 4 (2024): 651–62.

Downie, Jonathan. *Multilingual Church: Strategies for Making Disciples in All Languages*. William Carey, 2024.

Drury, Elizabeth. "Leading the Multiethnic Church: Help from New Metaphors and the Leadership Challenge." *Great Commission Research Journal* 2, no. 2 (2011): 205–20.

Duncum, Ian, Miriam Pepper, Nicole Hancock, and Ruth Powell. "A Comparison of the Vitality of Monocultural and Multicultural Churches: NCLS Research Occasional Paper 24." NCLS Research, May 2014. https://www.researchgate.net/publication/273260440_A_comparison_of_the_vitality_of_monocultural_and_multicultural_churches_NCLS_Occasional_Paper_24.

Dunlow, Jacob. "Disciples of All Nations: The Challenge of Nurturing Faith in Multi-Ethnic Congregations." *Christian Education Journal: Research on Educational Ministry* 14, no. 2 (2017): 285–305.

Dunn, Rick. "A 'New' Vision for Multi-Sites." GLI Church Planting. Accessed August 4, 2025. https://www.glichurchplanting.com/new-vision-multi-sites/.

Eastham, Karen. "Multicultural Children's Ministry." In *Multicultural Ministry Handbook: Connecting Creatively to a Diverse World*. Edited by David Anderson and Margarita Cabellon. InterVarsity, 2010.

Easum, William, and Dave Travis. *Beyond the Box: Innovative Churches That Work*. Group, 2003.

Edwards, Korie Little. *The Elusive Dream: The Power of Race in Interracial Churches*. Oxford University Press, 2008.

Edwards, Korie Little. "The Multiethnic Church Movement Hasn't Lived Up to Its Promise." *Christianity Today*, March, 2021. https://www.christianitytoday.com/2021/02/race-diversity-multiethnic-church-movement-promise/.

Edwards, Korie Little, and Rebecca Y. Kim. *Estranged Pioneers: Race, Faith, and Leadership in a Diverse World*. Oxford University Press, 2024.

Emerson, Michael O. "A New Day for Multiracial Congregations." *Reflections*. Accessed August 4, 2025. https://reflections.yale.edu/article/future-race/new-day-multiracial-congregations.

Emerson, Michael O. *People of the Dream: Multiracial Congregations in the United States*. Princeton University Press, 2006.

Emmanuel Gospel Center. "Shared Worship Space: An Urban Challenge and a Kingdom Opportunity." *Emmanuel Research Review* 74 (January 2012). https://www.egc.org/blog-2/2012/1/16/shared-worship-space-an-urban-challenge-and-a-kingdom-opportunity.

First Baptist Duluth. "Sunday Worship Gathering." YouTube, January 26, 2025. https://www.youtube.com/watch?v=BMopQJhVNbk.

Foster, Charles R. *Embracing Diversity: Leadership in Multicultural Congregations*. Alban Institute, 1997.

Galadima, Bulus, and Sam George. *Africans in Diaspora and Diasporas in Africa*. Langham Global, 2024.

Gjelton, Tom. "Multiracial Congregations May Not Bridge Racial Divide." *All Things Considered*, NPR, July 17, 2020. https://www.npr.org/2020/07/17/891600067/multiracial-congregations-may-not-bridge-racial-divide.

Gray, Derwin. *Building a Multiethnic Church: A Gospel Vision of Love, Grace, and Reconciliation in a Divided World*. Nelson, 2021.

Gray, Derwin. *The High-Definition Leader: Building Multiethnic Churches in a Multiethnic World*. Nelson, 2015.

Gushiken, Kevin M. "Cultivating Healthy Discipleship Settings in Multi-ethnic Churches." *Transformation: An International Journal of Holistic Mission Studies* 32, no. 1 (2015): 17–26.

Gushiken, Kevin M. "Is a Christian Identity Compatible with an Ethnic Identity? An Exploration of Ethnic Identity Negotiation Influences and Implications for Multi-Ethnic Congregations." *Christian Education Journal* 11, no. 1 (2014): 33–44.

Hammett, John S. "What Makes a Multi-Site Church One Church?" *Great Commission Research Journal* 4, no. 1 (2012): 95–107.

Hamstra, Sam. "Why We Don't Want to Rent Space." Christian Reformed Church: The Network, April 24, 2014. https://network.crcna

.org/topic/leadership/pastors/financial-shalom/church-management/why-we-dont-want-rent-space.

Han, Hahrie. *Undivided: The Quest for Racial Solidarity in an American Church*. Knopf, 2024.

Hardison, Richard W. "A Theological Critique of the Multi-Ethnic Church Movement: 2000–2013." PhD diss., Southern Baptist Theological Seminary, 2014.

Harris, Paula, and Doug Schaupp. *Being White: Finding Our Place in a Multiethnic World*. InterVarsity, 2004.

Harrison, Rodney, Tom Cheyney, and Don Overstreet. *Spin-Off Churches: How One Church Successfully Plants Another*. B&H Academic, 2008.

Hearn, Mark. *Technicolor: Inspiring Your Church to Embrace Multicultural Ministry*. B&H, 2017.

Hillsong. "Racial Equity." Accessed August 4, 2025. https://hillsong.com/newsroom/blog/2022/09/hillsong-racial-diversity-equity-and-inclusion-update/.

Hong, Eunice. "Intergenerational Church Conflict in the Korean American Church." PhD diss., Biola University, 2010.

House, Brad, and Gregg Allison. *MultiChurch: Exploring the Future of Multisite*. Zondervan, 2017.

Huyser-Honig, Joan. "Four Essentials for Multicultural Worship." Calvin Institute of Christian Worship, October 9, 2015. https://worship.calvin.edu/resources/articles/four-essentials-multicultural-worship.

Hyun, Dan. 2017. "The Challenge and Blessing of a Multicultural Leadership Team." Lifeway Research, January 9, 2017. https://research.lifeway.com/2017/01/09/challenge-blessing-multicultural-leadership-team/.

Ince, Irwyn L., Jr. *The Beautiful Community: Unity, Diversity, and the Church at Its Best*. InterVarsity, 2015.

Jensen, Eric, et al. "The Chance That Two People Chosen at Random Are of Different Race or Ethnicity Groups Has Increased Since 2010." US Census Bureau, August 12, 2021. https://www.census.gov/library/stories/2021/08/2020-united-states-population-more-racially-ethnically-diverse-than-2010.html.

Kim, Matthew. *Preaching with Cultural Intelligence: Understanding the People Who Hear Our Sermons*. Baker Academic, 2017.

Koo, Byoung Ok. "Multicultural Congregations as Models for Mono-Cultural Korean Churches: Reaching Out to Non-Koreans in the United States." PhD diss., Asbury Theological Seminary, 2013.

Koo, Byoung Ok. *Transitioning from an Ethnic to a Multicultural Church: A Transformational Model*. Wipf & Stock, 2019.

Kreiss, Daniel, and Efrem Smith. *Church for Everyone: Building a Multi-Inclusive Community for Emerging Generations*. InterVarsity, 2024.

Kunhiyop, Samuel Waje. *African Christian Theology*. Zondervan, 2019.

Kwiyani, Harvey C. *Multicultural Kingdom: Ethnic Diversity, Mission and the Church*. SCM, 2020.

Leeman, Jonathan. "Theological Critique of Multi-Site: What Exactly Is a 'Church'?" 9Marks, September 30, 2010. https://www.9marks.org/article/theological-critique-multi-site-what-exactly-church/.

Lewis-Giggetts, Tracey M. *The Integrated Church: Authentic Multicultural Ministry*. Beacon Hill, 2011.

Lifeway Research. "Protestant Churchgoer Views on Ethnic Diversity: A Survey of 1,002 American Protestant Churchgoers." Accessed August 4, 2025. https://research.lifeway.com/wp-content/uploads/2023/02/Sept-2022-Ethnicity-Report-American-Churchgoer.pdf.

Lindsay, Drew. "Two Churches, Two Races, One Pastor: Can They Become One Congregation?" Religion News Service, January 24, 2025. https://religionnews.com/2025/01/24/two-churches-two-races-one-pastor-can-they-become-one-congregation/.

Martí, Gerardo. "Mosaic on Mission: Creativity, Community, and Catalytic Leadership in an Innovative, Metropolitan, Multi-Ethnic Church." PhD diss., University of Southern California, 2002.

Marzouk, Safwat. *Intercultural Church: A Biblical Vision for an Age of Migration*. Fortress, 2019.

Mathews, Kenneth A., and M. Sydney Park. *The Post-Racial Church: A Biblical Framework for Multiethnic Reconciliation*. Kregel, 2011.

Maverick City Music. "Júbilo." On *Venga tu Reino*. Tribl. Released October 1, 2021.

Mbandi, Paul Muindi. "Toward a Theological Understanding of the Unity of the Church in Relation to Ethnic Diversity." PhD diss., Trinity Evangelical Divinity School, 2004.

McKay, Sherrie. "Episode 2: Language Songs 101." YouTube, December 21, 2021. https://www.youtube.com/watch?v=AqVzXZB4dbs.

McKay, Sherrie. "Multicultural Worship Arts Ministry: Transitioning from Monocultural Worship to a Multiethnic Worshiping Community." DMin diss., Nazarene Theological Seminary, 2022.

McNeil, Brenda Salter. *Roadmap to Reconciliation: Moving Communities into Unity, Wholeness and Justice*. InterVarsity, 2015.

Methodist Theological School in Ohio. "Benefits of Space-Sharing." Accessed August 4, 2025. https://www.mtso.edu/academics/faculty/ongoing-faculty-projects/space-sharing-by-congregations/benefits-of-space-sharing/.

Morrison, Latasha. *Brown Faces, White Spaces: Confronting Systemic Racism to Bring Healing and Restoration*. WaterBrook, 2024.

Mullins, Mark. "The Life-Cycle of Ethnic Churches in Sociological Perspective." *Japanese Journal of Religious Studies* 14, no. 4 (1987): 321–34.

National Park Service. "California: Second Baptist Church." Accessed August 4, 2025. https://www.nps.gov/articles/000/california-second-baptist-church-los-angeles.htm.

Nehrbass, Kenneth. *Advanced Missiology: How to Study Missions in Credible and Useful Ways*. Cascade Books, 2021.

Nehrbass, Kenneth. *God's Image and Global Cultures: Integrating Faith and Culture in the Twenty-First Century*. Cascade Books, 2021.

New York Times. "Worship Hour Found Time of Segregation." November 4, 1952, p. 26, col. 1. https://timesmachine.nytimes.com/timesmachine/1952/11/04/issue.html.

Nicholas, Angela. "Managing Group Conflict in the Multicultural Church: An Exegetical Research Analysis of Ephesians 2:11–22." *Emerging Leadership Journeys* 13, no. 1 (2019): 53–66.

Northouse, Peter. *Leadership: Theory and Practice*. 8th ed. Sage, 2019.

Okubo, Mason Keiji. "Unity and Diversity: Being a Multicultural Church." *Concordia Journal* 42, no. 3 (2016): 203–10.

Ola, Joseph. "African Millennial Christians in the Diaspora and the Identity Question." *Anvil* 37, no. 3 (2021): 13–23.

Oliveto, Karen. "Ministry at the Margins." In *Intercultural Ministry: Hope for a Changing World*, edited by Grace Ji-Sun Kim and Jann Aldredge-Clanton. Judson, 2017.

Ortiz, Manuel. *One New People: Models for Developing a Multiethnic Church*. IVP Academic, 1996.

Padilla, René. *Misión Integral: Ensayos Sobre el Reino de Dios y la Iglesia*. Ediciones Kairos, 2015.

Pais, Jeremy F., Scott J. South, and Kyle Crowder. "White Flight Revisited: A Multiethnic Perspective on Neighborhood Out-Migration." *Population Research and Policy Review* 28, no. 3 (2009): 321–46.

Palinkas, Lawrence A., Sarah M. Horwitz, Carla A. Green, Jennifer P. Wisdom, Naihua Duan, and Kimberly Hoagwood. "Purposeful Sampling for Qualitative Data Collection and Analysis in Mixed Method Implementation Research." *Administration and Policy in Mental Health* 42, no. 5 (2015): 533–44.

Parrett, Gary. "Becoming a Culturally Sensitive Minister." In *A Many-Colored Kingdom: Multicultural Dynamics for Spiritual Formation*, edited by Elizabeth Conde-Frazier, S. Steve Kang, and Gary Parrett. Baker Academic, 2004.

Patten, Malcolm. *Leading a Multicultural Church*. SPCK, 2016.

Perkins, John. *One Blood: Parting Words to the Church on Race and Love*. Moody, 2018.

Pomroy, Grace Duddy. "Church Rental Property Q&A." Faith+Lead, November 20, 2023. https://faithlead.org/blog/church-rental-property-qa/.

Proskuneo Ministries. *Feast of Praise*. March 26, 2025. https://www.proskuneo.org/proskuneo-store/p/feast-of-praise-live-album.

Rah, Soong-Chan. *Many Colors: Cultural Intelligence for a Changing Church*. Moody, 2010.

Redeeming Babel. "The After Party." Video course. https://redeemingbabel.org/the-after-party/free-course/.

Rhodes, Stephen A. *Where the Nations Meet: The Church in a Multicultural World*. InterVarsity, 1998.

Roberts, Laura. "Diversity in Worship: Applying a Process for Artistic Multicultural Practices in Emerging Multiethnic Church Plants." *Ethnodoxology* 12 (2024): A75–A89. https://artsandchristianfaith.org/index.php/journal/article/view/223.

Rodriguez, Daniel. *A Future for the Latino Church: Models for Multilingual, Multigenerational Hispanic Congregations*. IVP Academic, 2011.

Schaller, Lyle. *Innovations in Ministry: Models for the 21st Century*. Abingdon, 1994.

Seying, Kou. "Diversity and Unity in a Multicultural Church: God's Dream for the Twenty-First Century." *Concordia Journal* 42, no. 3 (2016): 193–202.

Shin, Sarah. *Beyond Colorblind: Redeeming Our Ethnic Journey*. InterVarsity, 2017.

Sinach. "Way Maker." On *Way Maker (Live)*. SLIC Inspire. November 2016.

Smith, Christine. "Laying a Foundation for a True and Viable Intercultural Church." In *Intercultural Ministry: Hope for a Changing World*, edited by Grace Ji-Sun Kim and Jann Aldredge-Clanton. Judson, 2017.

Snow, Martyn. *An Intercultural Church for a Multicultural World: Reflections on Gift Exchange*. Church House, 2024.

Sojourn Church. "Gospel, Race, and Injustice." Accessed August 4, 2025. www.sojournchurch.com/midtown/justice.

Solis, Gustavo, et al. "Why Activism Thrives in L.A.'s Black Churches." USC Today, February 7, 2022. https://today.usc.edu/black-church-change-social-justice-activism-usc/.

Steffen, Tom, and Cameron Armstrong, eds. *New and Old Horizons in the Orality Movement: Expanding the Firm Foundations*. Pickwick, 2022.

Stroupe, Nibs, and Inez Fleming. *While We Run This Race: Confronting the Power of Racism in a Southern Church*. Orbis Books, 1995.

Surratt, Geoff, Greg Ligon, and Warren Bird. *The Multi-Site Church Revolution: Being One Church in Many Locations*. Zondervan, 2006.

Taylor, Dan. "Pastoral Care and Education." In *Multicultural Ministry Handbook: Connecting Creatively to a Diverse World*, edited by David Anderson and Margarita Cabellon. InterVarsity, 2010.

Tennent, Timothy. *Theology in the Context of World Christianity: How the Global Church Is Influencing the Way We Think About and Discuss Theology*. Zondervan, 2007.

Tisby, Jemar. *The Color of Compromise: The Truth About the American Church's Complicity in Racism*. Zondervan, 2019.

Tomlin, Chris, Jason Ingram, Brian Johnson, Jenn Johnson, and Phil Wickham. "Holy Forever." On *Always*, by Chris Tomlin. Sparrow Records. 2022.

Van Opstal, Sandra. *The Next Worship: Glorifying God in a Diverse World*. InterVarsity, 2016.

Vaughn, Brad. *Reading Romans with Eastern Eyes: Honor and Shame in Paul's Message and Mission*. IVP Academic, 2019.

Volf, Miroslav. *Exclusion and Embrace: A Theological Exploration of Identity, Otherness, and Reconciliation*. Abingdon, 1996.

Wadsworth, Nancy D. *Ambivalent Miracles: Evangelicals and the Politics of Racial Healing*. University of Virginia Press, 2014.

Walls, Andrew. *The Cross-Cultural Process in Christian History*. Orbis Books, 2002.

Watkins, Keith. "Multi-Language Congregations: A Field Study in Los Angeles 1993." *Encounter* 55 (1994): 129–53.

White, Thomas, and Jon Mark Yeats. *Franchising McChurch: Feeding Our Obsession with Easy Christianity*. Cook, 2009.

Wickham, Phil, and Jonas Myrin. "Great Things." On *Living Hope*, by Phil Wickham. Fair Trade Services. 2018.

Williams, Jamaal E., and Timothy Paul Jones. *In Church as It Is in Heaven: Cultivating a Multiethnic Kingdom Culture*. InterVarsity, 2023.

Wise, David. "Developing a Genuinely Multi-Ethnic Local Church Congregation: An Auto-Ethnographic Investigation into Greenford Baptist Church, 1987–2014." DTh diss., University of Roehampton, 2022.

Yancey, George. *One Body, One Spirit: Principles of Successful Multiracial Churches*. InterVarsity, 2003.

Younker, Brett, Karl Martin, Kirby Kaple, Matt Redman, and Pat Barrett. "Build My Life." On *Pat Barrett*, by Pat Barrett. Sparrow Records. 2018.

Youssef, Fikri. "Bilingual Preaching: A Proposed Methodology for Multicultural Churches." DMin diss., Asbury Theological Seminary, 2023.

Index